secrets from a

Vegetarian
kitchen

secrets from a

Vegetarian
kitchen

NADINE ABENSUR

STEWART, TABORI & CHANG
New York

Text and recipes © 1996 by Nadine Abensur
The moral right of the author has been asserted
Photography © 1996 by Gus Filgate
Home Economist: Louise Pickford
Stylist: Penny Markham

Published and distributed in the U.S. in 1997 by
Stewart, Tabori & Chang,
a division of U.S. Media Holdings, Inc.
575 Broadway, New York, NY 10012

A Pavilion Book

Library of Congress Catalog Card Number: 96–71424

Designed by Wherefore Art?

Typeset in Neue Helvetica
Printed and bound in the United Arab Emirates

10 9 8 7 6 5 4 3 2 1

First Edition

contents

Tales From A Small Kitchen

My kitchen is tiny but you would never have guessed by the vast quantity of food that comes out of it—peach and almond tarts, moist and fragrant with Calvados, pastas and pestos, pungent with pounded olives, evocative of warm and lazier days, meringues, crisp and light, gooey and soft, all in the right degree, flavored delicately, romantically, with rose water, lavished with crystallized rose petals, light as a veil.

Mediterranean flavors one day and Middle Eastern ones the next. French for a very special occasion and pragmatic, down-to-earth stir-fries, produced in abundant quantities, for friends and last-minute suppers.

In my cooking, memories of India—slow, intense, vibrant, and ancient—and in my blood, the magical mystique of Morocco—a magical marriage of cumin and coriander; massive marmites of native olives, patiently pitted and slowly softened with whole lemons; masses of garlic, and golden brown onions. Memories, too, of big juicy, bright, bright red tomatoes, cut into large chunks, lightly salted, and garnished with the finest diced onion in the world and, as if that were not enough, then eaten on a terrace overlooking the wild Atlantic sea. These are some of the memories from a French, Jewish, Moroccan childhood, spent during the dying days of colonial splendor.

I remember tray upon tray of vivid canapés, deftly and nimbly put together by old aunts in preparation for some festivity. Untrained, yet skilled as any maestro, they sat on low woven stools, unselfconsciously chatting, laughing, dipping their fingers into ice-cold water before shaping the hot nougatine into little baskets for perfect marzipan fruit. I was thrilled. Then there was the unlikely delight of prune, onion, and almond confit, too sophisticated you might think for an eight-year-old, but I loved it. And imagine, a confit of miniature, jewel-like eggplants, regal in their deep purple skins, exotically drenched in glistening sugar syrup, or winter vegetables, not just roasted but caramelized, with the sweet gentle smell of cinnamon wafting through the open terraces.

All this, subconsciously imbibed, left me with an awareness of food too strong to ignore. Combined with a fascination with psychology, philosophy, art, and Eastern mysticism, this interest in food ultimately led me to a career devoted to the elevation of vegetarian cooking above its humble and ideologic beginnings....I am vegetarian because I *love* vegetables. I find them beautiful to look at. I revel in the smell of them, the feel of them, in their fabulous colors, and in the million and one ways in which they can be combined.

I am happy that vegetable cooking has come into its own and that its appreciation is causing a culinary revolution, the impact of which will eventually be felt on a level much deeper than culinary. We are becoming more sensitive to our ecology and to the fine balance in which it hangs. Seeing a wild berry bush is not commonplace. It is a moment of celebration and gratitude. Eating the fruits of the earth, when we think about it, is of a significance that is almost poignant.

Our passion for food grows in an attempt to make a connection with nature amid our concrete jungle.

If even one more person begins to appreciate vegetable cooking as a result of this book, or indeed is tempted back into the kitchen at all and even once experiences this very direct and creative link with nature, it will all have been worth it.

I would like to thank my parents for their sensitive palate; for their generosity of spirit and their wonderful sense of abundance; for knowing how to give without restraint; and for their joint forays in the kitchen, sometimes into the small hours of the night, concocting many a splendid thing, while we three children slept upstairs.

I am grateful to my friends, Dianna, Alankar, Jenny, Laura, Nitya, Mary, Robbie, Gyan, Shabda, and many others for their love and for being such willing and appreciative testers and tasters. Many thanks also to Sujan for his support in running Culinary Arts and his friendship in a year when I do not know how I would have survived without him, to Jack for his wit, brilliance, and inspired proddings in the kitchen, and to anyone who has in any way been a part of my life and contributed knowingly or unknowingly to this book.

My thanks to Chris Curry and everyone at Cranks and John Midgely of Pavilion Books, and finally to my long-suffering editor, Julia Canning, for her perseverance and skill.

Nadine Abensur

Ways To Cook a Vegetable

Braising In keeping with my French-Moroccan upbringing, I find braising the most delicious of all methods for cooking vegetables. Braising, which is halfway between frying and boiling, results in gentle tastes with all the inherent sweetness of the vegetables coaxed out. This is not an *al dente* method but the vegetables are melt-in-the-mouth without any of the sogginess and tastelessness of boiled ones. Braising turns the simplest vegetable almost into a meal. This is a method that does not fear the use of oil—the ratio is approximately 1 part oil to 3 parts water. A little sliced garlic, a few fresh herbs, and a pan with a heavy lid are the only other things that you need. Bring the liquid to a boil, reduce the heat, and simmer for 15–40 minutes depending on the texture of vegetable.

Broiling There is barely a decent restaurant in London these days, or indeed in any city for that matter, that has not been serving vegetables broiled, at their simplest—under a conventional broiler or, when you are lucky, over a charcoal grill or griddle—until the vegetables are charred and blackened and quite delicious. I have a small barbecue that I keep on my roof terrace and, as often as I can, I indulge in this slow and convivial cooking method.

The fashion for broiling bell peppers, then peeling them when the skins have charred and fallen away, is a wonderful way of enjoying the sweetness and succulence of the bell pepper's flesh, without the inconvenience of the indigestible skin. In Morocco and elsewhere in the Mediterranean, bell peppers are nearly always served this way and now this treatment of bell peppers is catching on elsewhere.

As more and more vegetables reach us from around the world, we become familiar with the cooking methods best suited to them. Nearly everyone's cooking vocabulary is expanding.

For best results, cut the vegetable you are using into slices, baste on both sides with a little olive oil, some crushed garlic, and some freshly ground sea salt. Place under a preheated broiler and turn over so both sides are browned and speckled with black.

Roasting Roasting is not confined, as too often thought, to potatoes and once a year to parsnips. Pearl onions, or whole ones cut into quarters, fennel, mushrooms, carrots, leeks, squashes, and pumpkins, even soft vegetables, such as tomatoes, or leafy varieties, such as Belgian endive, lettuce hearts, and chunks of cabbage, can be subjected to the treatment.

Place your selection in a large roasting tray, baste with olive oil, herbs of your choice, some whole unpeeled garlic cloves, and salt and pepper and place in a preheated oven on its highest setting, for at least 45 minutes, by which time they will have released their sweet juices and combined to make a delicious sauce. You can add a tablespoon of water or brandy to deglaze the bottom of the tray and mop up the lot with soft chunks of warm bread.

Frying Vegetables can be briefly sautéed or stir-fried over a high heat with the minimum of oil, a little marinade made with tamari, a little crushed garlic, and a few drops of Tabasco. They can even be fried in an almost dry skillet heated until quite hot, wilted in the case of spinach, in no more than the moisture of the spinach itself, or charred as for broiled and skinned bell peppers. (Do not attempt this in a nonstick skillet—you will soon wear out the coating.)

Mushrooms fried with the smallest amount of oil and a drop of tamari will shrivel, their flavor intensify, their high water content evaporate, and their texture become chewy and substantial. Add them to omelettes and to large mixed leaf salads. Alternatively, pour olive oil over them, refrigerate overnight, and serve as an antipasto. When frying a mixture of vegetables, it is best to add one type of vegetable at a time, all the harder ones such as carrots first, the softer ones, such as mushrooms, last. Work quickly, stirring the vegetables around the skillet in tossing and turning movements, half throwing the vegetables into the air and catching them again in a swift and rhythmic flick.

Deep Frying Is there anyone out there, however pure, however health conscious, who can resist the crisp, savory, and fattening appeal of vegetables deep fried in batter? Judging by my observations, I think not. When I serve appetizers with drinks, vegetable tempura, admittedly made with the lightest of beer-based batters, outdoes every colorful and imaginative canapé on the menu.

Make sure your oil is very hot indeed to begin with and then turn it down slightly as you fry the vegetables or you will have a major disaster with oil frothing up and spilling all over the place. Then drain them on several layers of paper towels and serve piping hot with a selection of sauces for dipping—try avocado blended to a very smooth purée with a drop of water, or mayonnaise with crushed garlic and capers, or a tamari sauce with a little Tabasco, some fine fresh or pickled ginger, and a little garlic with a few drops of water added. Filo pastry parcels and cigars are also perfect deep fried.

Purées and Mash It is not only potatoes that can be mashed, but almost every vegetable you care to mention. First either blanch or braise until soft, then blend in a food processor (and if really committed, pass through a fine sieve), then add a little oil or some cream or butter. Experiment with different combinations. Eat as they are, hot or cold, or combine with beaten egg and bake in a bain-marie like savory custards.

Try creamed cauliflower or a purée of petit pois or a combination of the two. Try also various pulses, the obvious chickpea humus, but the less common fava beans or butter beans laced with olive oil and spiked with shredded fresh herbs. Serve them on bread as part of a light summer meal with several different salads.

Baking in Parcels Vegetables can also be wrapped in foil or wax paper and cooked in their own steam. Try combinations of baby potatoes, whole pearl onions, whole button mushrooms, and whole cloves of garlic, with a little sea salt and a little freshly ground black pepper. Bake for 45 minutes and serve in the parcel, the aromas released as you unwrap the parcel.

Steaming Steaming is an excellent way of cooking the more delicate vegetables such as asparagus. A gentle way of cooking, it also retains nutrients and is good for slimmers since it does not require any oil. Place the vegetables in a steamer. This can be made of bamboo or stainless steel. Then set above a pan of boiling water until tender but not soft.

Try tossing steamed vegetables in a warm vinaigrette with plenty of grain mustard, or a dressing with tamari and nori flakes, toasted sesame seeds, and a drop or two of sesame oil, or a fresh pesto, made by pounding pine nuts with olive oil and a mass of fresh basil or coriander or arugula or watercress.

Searing In this method, the vegetables are placed in a metal (preferably iron) pan or griddle over high heat to seal in the flavors. Just lightly brush the pan with oil, turn up the heat, and sauté the vegetables so that the flavors are "seized" and the surfaces are lightly blanched in places.

Unusual Ingredients

Arugula Forget the mean little sachets sold at exorbitant prices in supermarkets and grow your own. I grow it in window boxes and it spreads like wildfire, almost as green and abundant as in any French or Italian market. It has a peppery taste that is intensified in the bigger leaves. And arugula known by any other name is just as good. Find it as rucola, arugula, rughetta, roquette, or rokkha. Use in salads, soups, and pasta sauces.

Balsamic Vinegar This has joined olive oil in its cult status. And not surprisingly since, while many of the younger cheaper versions are aged in balsamic wooden vats for only a few years, some of the expensive ones have sat in their wooden caskets for up to 50 years. That makes a 10-year plan seem pretty childish don't you think? It is just wonderful in dressings, sauces, and marinades, and I like it so much, I've been known to down a mouthful—neat.

Basil Who hasn't stuck their nose in a bunch of fresh basil, inhaled deeply the sweet and soothing scent, and let out a satisfied relaxed sigh. Use it in salads, or let it infuse sauces. Handle it carefully though; it is as delicate in its leaf structure as it is intense in its flavor.

Cumin I buy large bags of cumin from Indian supermarkets where it is known as jeera. I know of no other cuisine that uses it to such effect though as the Moroccan. The recipes in this book all call for the powder rather than the seed. By coincidence, this favorite spice of mine is of the same umbelliferous family as fennel, my favorite vegetable. Both are flowering plants, where stalks of nearly equal length spring from a common center to form clusters called umbels.

Marsala Wine A fortified wine from Sicily, which can be sweet or dry. Usually used in desserts, it is also good in savory dishes (see page 50).

Mascarpone A thick, fresh cream cheese made from cow's milk, mascarpone is the base of the now legendary tiramisu and is a great foil to fruit pies and summer fruit.

Mozzarella This may be made with cow's milk or the rarer and more highly prized buffalo milk. The latter is richer and made into bigger cheeses. I marinate ordinary mozzarella in olive oil, crushed garlic, and a little freshly ground sea salt and black pepper, before adding it to salads.

Olive Oil A whole book could be written on this subject. For the purposes of this book, you should have readily available a rich green virgin olive oil from Tuscany, and a light and fruity one, with any luck from Liguria. I avoid particularly pungent ones, but this is a matter of taste and probably a legacy from a childhood in Morocco where the olive oil was not always of the best quality and was eschewed for lighter, less distracting oils. Italian and French olive oils reach a great height of sophistication, however. Make your own flavored oils, by pushing sprigs of fresh herbs into the bottles or perhaps small, bright red chilies or whole cloves of garlic.

Orange Blossom Water A dilution of a flower essence, it lends a delicate scent to pastries, syrups, and desserts.

Parmesan This is a hard and grainy pressed cheese made from partially skimmed cow's milk. It can be aged for between 1^1/$_2$ and 2 years. The older cheese fares better on soups and pastas, the younger one on leaf salads or as dessert cheese. It has a sweet, rather sharp taste and is better grated or sliced very finely.

Polenta Polenta is made from corn kernels and is a staple of Northern Italy. It is poured slowly into boiling water and cooked gently and patiently. Once cooked, it can be spread out on a tray, cut into triangles, and broiled, or it may be eaten soft, right out of the pan. It is wonderful with Parmesan and with rich and intense sauces.

Rose Water I can understand that rose water and essence is reputed to be good for the heart (the emotional heart that is), with healing and antidepressive properties. Certainly, in moments of grief, I have filled my house with fragrant, scented roses and added the oil (which is worth its weight in gold) to baths and felt much uplifted.

Rose water is made from diluted rose petal essence. It is used in Middle Eastern desserts and I prefer it when its effect is perceptible but subtle. Rosa damascena is the rose grown in Morocco (and also in Bulgaria and India) with thickly textured petals that retain their fragrance well when dried. Buy the purest rose water you can, from a reputable herbalist.

Sun-dried Tomatoes In my next incarnation, I will live on a sun-drenched terrace overlooking a vast sea and I will cut, salt, and place on drying racks the tomatoes grown on my own vines. And I will look at them every day until they are shriveled and shrunk, then I will pick one and eat it right there and then, while it is still soft, still warm.

Buy your own dried tomatoes, reconstitute them in water for several hours and marinate them yourself in olive oil and fresh basil or oregano with a little salt and pepper. This way you avoid the vinegary taste of most ready-soaked ones. Blend them with added olive oil and the merest touch of sugar for a versatile sun-dried tomato paste.

Tamari Tamari is another versatile ingredient of Japanese origin and is the purest of soy sauces made entirely from the fermentation of soybeans and with no added wheat. Soy sauce on the other hand is made from equal parts of soybeans and wheat. I tend to use tamari but there are several varieties of soy sauces and tamari available and you might like to experiment. Some are thick and syrupy and almost sweet. Others are much lighter and clearer. Both are wonderful added to sauces and soups of any nationality. In creating vegetarian recipes, I do not know where I would be without tamari.

Tofu The word tofu usually has those who have heard about it screw their noses up in displeasure. This is a great shame. True, it has no distinguishable flavor of its own and has a rather unprepossessing appearance. But it has such potential! Made from soy milk, almost any flavor can be imparted to it. It is a Japanese ingredient but it can take on French, Moroccan, Italian, Thai, Spanish—you name it—characteristics. You can marinate it, mince it, sear it, and deep fry it. You can stuff it, roast it, and freeze it. Be generous with strong seasoning. It is a natural ally of tamari. It loves wine, especially red. It is elevated by garlic and ginger. It likes anything with a high salt content but is as easily sweetened. It is very effectively smoked. It is very low fat. It is great on brochettes and kebabs and I have included it in several of my recipes.

Umeboshi Plums These are Japanese plums gathered in mountain orchards, pickled with Shiso (perilla) leaves and salt, and then sun-dried. They can be turned into a paste or into Ume Su, a vinegar that can be added to stir-fries and salads.

Light Vegetable Stock

This is for use in pale and delicate soups, such as Cream of Fennel and Almond Soup or Summer Risotto, and in all white wine based sauces. A little bouillon powder added to stock gives it added flavor. Do not add any dark-colored vegetables. If you are short of time, you can substitute stock made with a stock cube but obviously the flavor will not be as good.

Makes 1 qt./1 lt
- 2 tbsp. butter
- 1 celery stalk, chopped
- 1 head fennel, chopped
- 1 large onion, chopped
- 6 garlic cloves, crushed
- 2 carrots, chopped
- 1 zucchini, sliced
- 1 tsp. bouillon powder, or salt if not available
- 1 chunk of peeled celeriac, chopped
- ¼ cup/60 ml white wine
- white pepper, to taste

Heat the butter in a large heavy-based saucepan, add the vegetables and cook until soft. Add the wine and cook for a few more minutes. Cover with water and simmer for 45 minutes. Strain and, when cool, skim off the surface fat and discard. This is at its best when very fresh, but can be stored in the refrigerator for up to 2 days.

Sun-dried Tomato Pesto

Couldn't you eat this every day for a week, mixed with a different pasta each time? Lazy cook or creature of habit, I often do.

Serves 6
- 1½ tbsp. sun-dried tomatoes, drained of oil and water
- 2 tbsp. finely chopped fresh parsley
- 1½ tbsp. pitted black olives
- 2 tbsp. pine nuts
- 2 shallots, chopped
- 2 garlic cloves, crushed
- 1 tbsp. lemon juice
- salt and pepper, to taste
- 4 tbsp. olive oil
- 1 tbsp. freshly grated Parmesan cheese

Place all the ingredients, except the oil and Parmesan, in a food processor and blend for 30 seconds or until roughly chopped. Slowly pour in the oil and blend until smooth. Stir in the Parmesan at the very end or reserve and add separately when mixing with pasta.

Dark Vegetable Stock

This is a particularly rich stock for use in dark sauces and soups, especially those containing red wine or tamari. It is good added to mushroom fricassé, brilliant in French onion soup, and makes a meal in itself with a spoonful of miso and a handful of egg noodles. Much of the world's most refined soups and sauces depend on good fresh stock but this is invariably meat-based. You will find this stock as deep and rich as you could wish.

1 small cauliflower, divided into flowerets
5–6 brocolli flowerets
3 carrots, chopped
5–6 mushrooms,
preferably dark strong-flavored ones, sliced
1 celery stalk, chopped
1 large onion, chopped
6 garlic cloves, crushed
3–4 scallions, sliced
2 zucchini, sliced
1 tomato, chopped
3–4 bay leaves
3–4 basil leaves
2 tbsp. brown lentils

Makes 1 qt./1 lt

Place all the ingredients in a large heavy-based saucepan. Cover with water and bring to a boil. Simmer gently for at least 1 hour, preferably 2, then strain and use as needed. Store for up to 1 day in the refrigerator.

Fresh Tomato Sauce

Only attempt this in the summer, with the reddest, tastiest tomatoes you can find. My local grocer always has plenty of crimson vine tomatoes which I like to use. Plum tomatoes, which are no longer the rarity they were, are also good when they are fresh and ripe enough.

Serves 6–8 4 lb./2.2 kg/about 16 ripe, firm red tomatoes
$\frac{1}{2}$ cup/120 ml fruity olive oil
1 large onion, diced
4–6 garlic cloves, peeled
1 small bunch fresh basil,
   left on the stalk with a few leaves reserved
1 tsp. tomato paste or sun-dried tomato paste (see page 11)
$\frac{1}{2}$ tsp. superfine sugar
salt and pepper, to taste

Bring a large pan of salted water to a boil and plunge in the tomatoes for about 1 minute until all the skins are split. Drain immediately and, when cool, remove the skins and seeds. (I do this over a sieve placed over a pan to catch the escaping juices, which I then add to the tomatoes.)

Meanwhile, heat the oil and fry the diced onion until transparent. Throw in the tomatoes and juice and break up with a potato masher. Add the whole garlic, basil, tomato paste, sugar, and salt and pepper. Bring to a boil, then reduce to a steady simmer and cook uncovered for at least 1 hour. Depending on how much juice you have succeeded in retaining, you may find that the sauce takes up to 2–2$\frac{1}{2}$ hours to reduce down to a thick, rich consistency.

Remove and discard the whole garlic cloves and basil, which will have released all their sweetness. Serve the sauce as it is, or blend in a food processor for a smoother consistency.

Tear several fresh basil leaves and add at the last minute.

Harissa

Harissa is a fiery red sauce that I've seen bring tears to people's eyes. Cumin is not absolutely typical of it but I like it so much that I often add a little to the usual ingredients. I also sometimes add a little ketchup, which provides a soothing sweetness. You can of course modify the quantity of chili to your taste.

8 oz./250 g/1 cup dried fiery red chili peppers
1 medium-sized whole head garlic
1 tbsp. dried coriander
1 tbsp. caraway or fennel seeds
1 tbsp. fresh mint, finely chopped
3 tbsp. or more fresh coriander leaves

Makes 1³/₄ cups/420 ml

1 tsp. cumin (optional)
1 tsp. tomato ketchup
  (optional)
1 tbsp. salt
1 tbsp. olive oil

Remove stems and seeds from the chilies and soak in water for 1 hour. Drain and pound with a pestle and mortar with the garlic, coriander, caraway or fennel seeds, mint, coriander leaves, cumin, and ketchup (if using), and salt, moistening with a little olive oil, to obtain a thick paste. Use extremely sparingly. It is often served as an accompaniment to couscous (see *Couscous Royale*, page 90) and to *Harira* (see page 22) and it can also be added to sauces and to mayonnaise.

Basic Pie Pastry

This is a very short pastry with over half the amount of butter to flour but it is not too difficult to handle. Use very cold water to bind it and work with light airy movements of your fingers.

1⁴/₅ cup all-purpose flour
1 stick unsalted butter
¹/₂ cup confectioner's sugar
small pinch of salt
1 egg (optional)
approx. 2 tbsp. ice-cold water

Makes enough for a
12-inch/30-cm pastry
case

Put the flour on a work surface and make a well in the center. Cut the butter into small pieces, place them in the well, then work with your fingertips until completely softened. Add the sugar and salt, then the egg if using or just the cold water. Gradually draw the flour into the mixture until thoroughly incorporated. Work the dough a couple of times with the palm of your hand until it is very smooth.

Roll the dough into a ball, wrap in waxed paper, and refrigerate for at least 1 hour. Roll out on a floured surface and use as required.

Following pages: Red Bell Pepper Soup with Eggplant Caviar

Soups

Red Bell Pepper Soup *with* Eggplant Caviar

I have seen this soup made with the addition of onions (which loses the wonderful intensity of color), with red lentils (which loses the wonderful intensity of flavor), and with tomatoes, which you might like to try, but this recipe is still by far my most favorite version because it produces a soup with a wonderfully vibrant color and an intense flavor. You may like to replace the eggplant "caviar" with a Provençale black olive tapenade—the black color of this garnish is very striking against the redness of the soup.

Serves 6

4 lb./2 kg/8 red bell peppers
1 garlic clove
5 cups /1.2 lt light
vegetable stock (see page 12)
dash of Tabasco sauce
salt

For the garnish
1 lb./450 g/1 large or 2 small eggplants,
   cut into ½-inch/1-cm chunks
¼ cup/60 ml olive oil
1 garlic clove, crushed
salt and pepper, to taste
1 cup/230 ml Greek yogurt or sour cream
2 scallions, green part only,
   finely chopped on the slant (optional)

To make the soup, place the bell peppers under a very hot broiler until the skins are charred on all sides. However, take care not to overcook the bell peppers—it is important that the flesh itself remains as red as possible and does not turn black. Discard any part of the flesh that may have become black.

Set aside the bell peppers to cool in a bowl covered with a cloth or plastic wrap so that the vapors rising from the heat loosen the skin from the flesh. Peel and remove all seeds and pith.

Blend the bell peppers in a food processor with the garlic, a little stock, a dash of Tabasco, and salt. Add the rest of the stock and heat to a gentle simmer.

To make the garnish, sprinkle the eggplant with salt and allow to drain for at least 1 hour to extract the bitter juices. Rinse well. Heat the olive oil in a skillet and add the eggplant, crushed garlic, and salt and pepper. Fry until completely soft but the blackness of the skins is still visible. Serve the soup warm or chilled, garnishing each serving, with a spoonful of eggplant "caviar," a spoonful of Greek yogurt or sour cream, and a few slivers of scallion if using.

Watercress Soup

I first made this soup for sixty people—picking the individual leaves off the stalk was a laborious job, as you can imagine. Cooking the soup for six is a much more enjoyable experience. The soup can be made the day before (without the cream) and refrigerated overnight. Do not store it for very long otherwise the flavor and color will be spoiled.

1¼ lb./600 g/6 cups watercress
1 stick butter
1 lb./450 g/3 cups potatoes, diced
salt and pepper, to taste
2 garlic cloves, cut into slivers
¼ cup/60 ml light cream
6 tbsp. heavy cream, crème fraîche, or
Carrot and Cashew Soup (see page 20), to garnish

Serves 6

For the stock
1 medium onion, sliced
3 scallions, sliced
6 medium green beans
3 celery-leaf sprigs
1 garlic clove, crushed
2 fresh basil leaves (optional)
3 pt./1.5 lt water

Remove the watercress leaves from the stalks and reserve the stalks for the stock.

To make the stock, place the onion, scallions, green beans, celery-leaf sprigs, garlic, reserved watercress stalks, and the basil, if using, in a large saucepan. Add the water and simmer for 1 hour. Strain and set aside.

Melt the butter in a heavy-bottomed saucepan. Add the potatoes and sauté gently for 10 minutes without allowing the potatoes to turn even the slightest bit brown. Add salt and pepper and stir.

Add the watercress leaves, a handful at a time, then add one ladle of stock and the garlic. Stir, cover, and simmer over a low heat for 10 minutes, stirring often and adding a little more stock if there is any danger of sticking. Blend in a food processor until completely smooth, then pass through a fine sieve.

Return to the pan, add the rest of the stock and stir well. Bring back to a very gentle boil and only then add the light cream. Remove from the heat immediately and serve.

Garnish each serving with a swirl of heavy cream or crème fraîche or a spoonful of *Carrot and Cashew Soup* (page 20), poured at one side like a rising sun.

Fennel *and* Almond Soup *with* Cardamom

When I first came to England, I missed my friends, not surprisingly for an eight-year-old! I missed the brilliant sunshine and I missed… fennel. I had memories of it piled up high in noisy, magnificent Arab markets, taken home in large rope bags, then braised very slowly and gently. It was, and still is, my favorite vegetable.

It was to be ten years before I saw fennel again, by which time England was finally part of the European Common Market and hitherto forgotten vegetables were beginning to make a tentative comeback. I was so happy I cried! Now I eat it in that old familiar way—braised and soft and soothingly sweet—but I also enjoy it in soups, here elevated to the exotic with the addition of cardamom.

Choose perfect, white, unblemished bulbs with the outer skin still intact. The fresher the fennel, the better the flavor.

Serves 6   2 tbsp. sunflower oil
1 small onion or shallot, finely sliced
1¼ lb./600 g/3 fennel bulbs, quartered,
    with the green leaves reserved for garnish
2 garlic cloves
5 cardamom pods
2½ cups/600 ml water
1 tsp. bouillon powder (½ veg stock cube)
1 oz./25 g/1 heaped tbsp. ground almonds
2 tbsp. heavy cream
salt and pepper, to taste

Heat the sunflower oil in a skillet, add the sliced onion and fry until transparent. Add the fennel quarters, garlic cloves, and the seeds scraped out of the cardamom pods. Then add half the water and the bouillon powder. Cover with a lid. Bring to a boil and simmer gently for 15 minutes.

Now add the rest of the water and the ground almonds and stir until very smooth. For a really smooth texture, you can always sieve the mixture at this point. Stir in the cream, add salt and pepper to taste, then serve, garnishing each bowl with the finely chopped fennel leaves.

Carrot *and* Cashew Soup

This soup is child's play to make and is kept deliberately gentle on the seasoning. It is absolutely delicious in its simplicity. It is worth making a double batch (which makes it easier to blend the cashews) and freezing half.

Serves 6   1 small onion, cut into quarters
12 oz./350 g/2½ cups medium carrots, sliced into
    ¼-inch/½-cm rounds
1¼ cups/300 ml light vegetable stock (see page 12)
1 oz./25 g/⅕ cup whole unsalted cashews
salt and pepper, to taste

Place the onion and carrots in a saucepan with the stock. Cover with a lid, bring to a boil, and simmer until completely tender. Set aside.

Blend the cashews in a food processor with a little stock until smooth as a purée without any gritty bits left in it. Add the onion and carrot mixture and blend to make a very smooth and velvety soup. Pass through a fine sieve for a completely smooth texture. Season with salt, but allow guests to add their own black pepper.

Split Pea *and* Mushroom Soup

In my impoverished student days, I made large batches of this soup to sell in poly-styrene cups to stall holders and browsers at bohemian open-air markets. Dozens of portions would sell in minutes and I built up a regular clientele for an entire winter. It is another example of ingredients brought to life by cumin in simple Moroccan fashion.

1 tbsp. olive oil   Serves 6–8
1 medium onion, diced
1 lb./450 g/2¼ cups green split peas
3 garlic cloves, left whole
1 heaped tsp. cumin powder
6 cups/1.5 lt dark vegetable stock (see page 13)
1 tbsp. tamari (plus a dash for the mushrooms)
Tabasco sauce, to taste
salt and pepper, to taste
4 oz./100 g/2 cups button mushrooms, sliced

Heat the oil in a pressure cooker pan and fry the onion until soft. Add the split peas, whole garlic, cumin, and vegetable stock and cook under medium pressure for 10 minutes. Blend in a liquidizer or food processor, then add the tamari and season with Tabasco, salt and pepper to taste. In a separate and almost dry pan, fry the mushrooms, with just a dash of tamari and Tabasco, until slightly dried out and crisply browned. Add to the soup and serve.

Cannellini Bean Soup *with* Arugula *and* Saffron

A friend gave me an aromatic lemon-flavored olive oil as a birthday gift. It must have been intended for this soup. In the absence of such spoils, simply add half a whole lemon cut into chunks to the simmering soup to add that sour succulence. Do not let impatience goad you into adding the arugula until the last possible moment. Green leaves of all kinds require the very briefest of heat otherwise they oxidize, blacken, and ruin what should be bright and verdant.

6 saffron strands   Serves 6
2 tbsp. olive oil or lemon olive oil
10 oz./300 g/2 cups onion, diced   ½ lemon (optional)
1 tsp. bouillon powder   1 tsp. grain mustard
1 celery stalk, finely sliced   10 oz./300 g/2½ bunches
2 14-oz./400-g cans/1¾ cups cannellini beans   arugula
4 garlic cloves   salt and pepper, to taste

Infuse the saffron in 2 tbsp. of hot water and set aside for 10 minutes until the water is a deep rusty color.

Heat the lemon oil in a saucepan, add the onion and fry gently until soft. Add the bouillon powder and the finely sliced celery and cook until transparent. Add the cannellini beans with their liquid, as well as the whole garlic cloves. Cut the lemon into quarters (if using) and add to the pan with the mustard.

Bring to a boil, then simmer for 10 minutes. Just before serving, remove the lemon and reheat. Add the saffron water and arugula, either whole or roughly torn, then season with salt and pepper. Remove from the heat and serve at once.

Harira

When I was a child living in Morocco, I remember during Ramadan (the Muslim month of fasting) sharing the excitement at sunset when those fasting were permitted to feast on this rich and nourishing chick-pea soup. Ever since then chick-peas have remained one of my favorite foods. This recipe comes from Morocco via Washington, and although it originally contained meat, none of its richness has been lost.

Serves 6
¼ cup/60 ml sunflower oil
4 oz./100 g/¾ cup onion, chopped
4 oz./100 g/½ cup brown lentils
4 oz./100 g/½ cup chick-peas, soaked overnight
4 oz./100 g/½ cup dried fava beans, soaked
1 lb./450 g/3¼ cups fresh tomatoes, chopped
1 head celery, including green leaves
6 saffron strands, soaked in 2 tbsp. of hot water for 10 minutes
salt and pepper, to taste
2½ qt./2.25 lt water
2 tbsp. all-purpose flour
1 large bunch parsley, finely chopped
1 large bunch coriander, finely chopped
juice of 1½ lemons

Heat the oil in a saucepan, add the onion and fry until transparent. Add the lentils and cook for a few minutes continuously stirring. Then add the chick-peas and the fava beans as well as the tomatoes, celery, saffron, and pepper to taste. Cover with the water. Simmer, covered, for at least an hour or until the chick-peas and beans are very tender. Add salt only when the chick-peas and fava beans have begun to soften.

Mix the flour with a little water, just enough to make a smooth paste. Pour in a ladle of hot soup, beat well to avoid lumps and pour back into the pan. Bring to a boil and cook, stirring vigorously, until the soup thickens. Add the parsley and coriander.

Remove the pan from the heat, then add the lemon juice. Serve at once.

Fresh Tomato Soup *with* Sun-dried Tomato Paste

I haven't yet met any of those rare beings who don't like fresh tomato soup and although this soup is for true connoisseurs, I know it tempts everyone. Eat it hot or cold, with a dollop of crème fraîche or one or two pieces of mozzarella. For more delectation, melt the mozzarella on a circle of toast and float it on the soup—a perfect balance of crisp and smooth textures, strong and gentle flavors. Use ripe summer tomatoes and let the sun-dried tomato paste add depth and pungency.

1/2 cup/120 ml light olive oil   **Serves 6**
8 oz./225 g/1²/₃ cups red onion, chopped
6 lb./3 kg/about 24 vine tomatoes (or good red, ripe tomatoes)
6 garlic cloves, left whole
several large basil leaves, on the stalk
1/2 tsp. superfine sugar
couple dashes of Tabasco sauce
salt and pepper
1 heaped tbsp. sun-dried tomato paste (see page 11)
6 tbsp. heavy cream
several tiny basil leaves, from the base of the plant

Heat the olive oil and add the finely diced red onion. Cook gently until transparent.

Plunge the tomatoes in boiling water and blanch for 1 minute or until the skins come away easily. Scrape away the flesh that clings to the skin since this has most of the flavor and color. Place the seeds in a colander and catch the juices. Place the flesh and juice in a food processor and blend for a few seconds. Pour into the pan with the onion and add the whole garlic, basil, sugar, Tabasco, and salt to taste. Bring to a boil and reduce gently for 15 minutes in which time the depth of color and flavor will have considerably intensified. About halfway through the cooking time, add the sun-dried tomato paste. Remove the garlic when it is totally soft but before it falls apart. At the same time, extract the basil leaves, which will be completely wilted and will have released their delicious sweetness into the soup. Stir in 1 tbsp. heavy cream.

Garnish each serving with a swirl of heavy cream, a scattering of tiny basil leaves, and freshly ground black pepper.

Following pages: Pumpkin Soup with Spinach

Borscht

One of these days I will carry out an experiment. If the world is divided into those who love beets and those who hate them, what else might we deduce about the politics, the religious beliefs, the psychological makeup of the individuals in these opposed camps? Before we find out, won't you join me in savoring a dish that can only be described as a beet lover's paradise?

Serves 6

- 2 lb./900 g/2²/₃ cups small beets
- 5 cups/1.2 lt water
- ¼ cup/60 ml sunflower oil
- 2 oz./50 g/½ cup onion, chopped
- 1 lb./450 g/2³/₄ cups medium potatoes, diced
- 3 oz./75 g/just over ½ cup medium carrots, sliced
- dash of Tabasco sauce
- ½ cup/120 ml vodka
- juice of 1 small lemon
- salt and pepper
- *For the garnish*
- ²/₃ cup/160 ml plain yogurt
- 1 tbsp. chopped fresh parsley
- 1 tbsp. chopped fresh dill

Place the beets in a pressure cooker with the water and cook at medium for 15 minutes, or in an ordinary pan with the lid on for 45 minutes or until tender. Drain the beets, reserving the cooking liquid. Allow the beets to cool, then slip the skins off and cut the flesh into quarters.

In a separate pan, heat the oil and fry the onion until transparent, then add the potato, carrot, and Tabasco and continue to fry for 5 minutes. Add the chopped beets and stir well for 2 minutes. Pour in the reserved beet cooking liquid and continue to cook for 10 minutes. A couple of minutes before the end of cooking time, add the vodka and lemon juice to the soup. Blend with a hand-held electric whisk or allow to cool, then blend in a food processor. Season with salt and pepper.

Serve the soup. Garnish each serving with a spoonful of yogurt and a sprinkling of parsley and dill.

Pumpkin Soup *with* Spinach

The seasoning in this soup is kept deliberately simple to enhance the unique taste of pumpkin. I love the contrast of the cold yogurt with the hot soup and would happily eat two bowls of this without anything else and call it a meal.

2¹/₂ lb./1.2 kg/8 cups pumpkin,   **Serves 6**
peeled and cut into 2 x 2-inch/5 x 5-cm chunks
1 large onion, cut into chunks
1 medium carrot, cut into chunks
3 garlic cloves
1 tsp. bouillon powder
1¹/₂ qt./1.5 lt water
¹/₄ cup/60 ml olive oil
1 tbsp. tamari
salt and pepper, to taste
4 oz./100 g/1¹/₂ cups baby spinach
1 tbsp. heavy cream (optional)
6 tbsp. Greek yogurt, to garnish

Place all the vegetables, garlic, and bouillon powder in a pan with the water and bring to a boil. Simmer gently for 20 minutes or until the vegetables are tender.

Blend in a food processor until very smooth, then return to the pan. Add the olive oil and tamari and season with salt and pepper. Throw in the spinach leaves and stir for 1 minute, adding the cream, if using.

Serve at once. Garnish each serving with a tablespoon of Greek yogurt.

Celeriac Soup *with* Lemongrass *and* Coriander

A juxtaposition of tastes, a merging of cultures—these are the pointers to modern eating. Europe, Asia, the Middle East…world cuisine in a bowl of soup.

2 lb./900 g/1 large head celeriac   **Serves 6**
4 oz./100 g/1 cup onion, chopped
4 oz./100 g/²/₃ cup potatoes, cut into chunks
3 garlic cloves
1 tsp. bouillon powder
¹/₄ cup/60 ml olive oil
2¹/₂ pt./1.2 lt water
1 stalk lemongrass
1 large coriander sprig, plus extra sprigs to garnish
2 tbsp. heavy cream

Place all the ingredients except the cream in a large saucepan and bring to a boil. Simmer for about 20 minutes until the vegetables are completely tender.

Remove the lemongrass and coriander and blend the remaining mixture in a food processor until very smooth. Pass through a fine sieve.

Return to the cleaned-out pan and bring to a boil. Add the cream, heat through for a minute longer and serve garnished with fresh coriander.

Following pages: Almond and Tofu Cigars with Green Olive Confit

Hot and Cold Starters

Baby Eggplants *with* Roasted Tomatoes, Feta Cheese, *and* Broiled Scallions

This starter, if you assemble it as described, is as pretty as a picture and light enough to be followed by more hearty fare. Use a soft young feta cheese (not too sharp or acidic), the brightest tomatoes, and the smallest, rounded baby eggplants.

Serves 6

9 baby eggplants
freshly ground sea salt and pepper, to taste
dash of Tabasco sauce
1 tsp. balsamic vinegar
1 bunch scallions, trimmed
$^1\!/_2$ yellow bell pepper
6 ripe medium vine tomatoes
1$^1\!/_2$ garlic cloves, crushed
1$^1\!/_2$ cups fresh breadcrumbs
$^1\!/_2$ cup/120 ml olive oil
1 tbsp. chopped fresh coriander
4 oz./100 g/1 cup feta cheese, cut into tiny cubes
15 whole roasted garlic cloves (see page 125)
1 tbsp. fresh coriander leaves, stalks removed

Heat the oven to 325°F/160°C. Cut the baby eggplants in half, sprinkle with a little salt and Tabasco and balsamic vinegar. Place under a very hot broiler for 4–5 minutes until golden brown and soft inside. Transfer to a plate and set aside.

Add the scallions to the broiler pan, baste with the pan juices, and broil for 3–4 minutes, turning at least once to make sure they don't burn.

Broil the yellow bell pepper until charred on all sides, remove the skin and cut into rough $^1\!/_2$-inch/1-cm squares.

Place the tomatoes on a cookie sheet with $^1\!/_2$ tsp. crushed garlic and a little salt. Bake in the oven for about 1 hour.

Mix the breadcrumbs with 2 tbsp. of olive oil, the remaining crushed garlic clove, and the chopped coriander. Increase the oven temperature to 425°F/220°C. Place the breadcrumb mixture on a cookie sheet and bake for 6–7 minutes until a pale golden color.

To serve, place a roasted tomato (served hot or cold) in the center of an individual plate. Prop three halves of eggplant around it and arrange feta cheese cubes around the edge. Scatter yellow bell pepper pieces here and there. Place 1 scallion on one side and sprinkle lightly with the toasted breadcrumbs. Finally, garnish with the roasted garlic cloves and a few coriander leaves strewn at random and drizzle a little olive oil over the top.

Fava Beans, New Potatoes, *and* Straw Mushrooms *on* Baby Spinach

It is not often that I find a use for canned or frozen goods, yet incredibly this delicious starter (you could also eat it as a main course) may make use of both. The Chinese straw mushrooms, which, unless you are very lucky, you will only find in cans, have a less distinctive taste than their unusual Russian doll appearance might suggest. They look like a mushroom within a mushroom and they absorb beautifully the cumin and olive oil. Fresh fava beans are a brief luxury of summer months and are worth all the fiddly preparation; however, frozen ones are invariably very good and can be used all year round—a fact you will appreciate when you taste this. Remember to add fresh or frozen beans only at the very last minute, folding them in gently.

½ cup/120 ml olive oil
1 heaped tbsp. paprika
1 tbsp. cumin
6 tbsp. water
2 garlic cloves, crushed
1 lb./450 g/2½ cups small new potatoes, boiled
6 oz./175 g/1 cup straw mushrooms
8 oz./225 g/1½ cups fava beans, blanched for 5 minutes and skins removed
salt and pepper, to taste
6 tbsp. sour cream, to garnish
For the spinach
1 lb./450 g/6 cups baby spinach
1 tbsp. olive oil
1 tsp. lemon juice

Serves 6

Heat the olive oil in a large skillet over a low heat. Add the paprika, cumin, and water and stir briskly over a low heat, so the spices do not burn but lose their powdery quality. Add a little more water if necessary. Add the garlic and continue to cook for 1 minute.

Add the new potatoes and stir gently for 1–2 minutes to coat well with the spices. Gently add the straw mushrooms and continue to cook for a further minute, moving the skillet around continually and avoiding any drying out or sticking. Turn off the heat and add the fava beans, folding them in gently, so that they do not break up. Season with salt and pepper.

Serve warm on a bed of baby spinach lightly tossed in olive oil and lemon juice. Garnish each serving with a spoonful of sour cream.

Following pages: Baby Eggplants with Roasted Tomatoes, Feta Cheese, and Broiled Scallions

Vegetable Sushi

Say the word sushi and everyone thinks "fish," but the sushi given here are of course all vegetable. Instead of making roll shapes, you can always form the seaweed into cones, a bit like pastry cream horns, and fill them with rice and vegetables. Let your imagination flow when creating fillings. Sushi make addictive cocktail party food or a sophisticated starter and look most impressive served in individual lacquer boxes.

Serves 6–8   1 lb./450 g/2 cups short-grain rice

1 1/4 pt./600 ml water

2 tbsp. clear malt vinegar

1 tbsp. superfine sugar

5–6 sheets nori seaweed

For the fillings:

1 tbsp. tamari or soy sauce

1 tsp. balsamic vinegar

1 tsp. Ume Su (optional)

1 garlic clove, crushed

1 red bell pepper

1 yellow bell pepper

1 medium zucchini, cut into matchstick strips

1 tbsp. mixed olive oil and sesame oil

8 oz./200 g/1 cup smoked tofu, cut into matchstick strips

1 tsp. sesame seeds

5–6 tsp. Umeboshi paste

For the dipping sauce:

1/2 cup/120 ml tamari diluted with 2 tbsp. water

dash of Tabasco sauce

small piece of pickled ginger or fresh ginger

2–3 slivers scallions, green part only,
    cut on the diagonal

1–2 very thinly sliced carrots

Make a marinade with half the soy sauce, the balsamic vinegar, Ume Su, and the garlic. Broil the red and yellow bell peppers until the skins are black. Peel and remove the seeds, then cut into strips. Add to the marinade along with the zucchini strips and set aside for about 1 hour.

Meanwhile, place the rice in a saucepan with the water. Bring to a boil, reduce the heat, and simmer for 12 minutes until the water has been absorbed. Remove from heat and stir in the malt vinegar and sugar. Leave to cool.

Heat the oils in a skillet and fry the tofu strips, adding the rest of the soy sauce and stirring continuously for 4–5 minutes until the tofu begins to crisp and brown. Finally, add the sesame seeds.

To make the dipping sauce, mix the diluted tamari with the Tabasco, ginger, scallions, and carrot slices.

To assemble, spread some of the cooled rice onto a sheet of seaweed, spreading it right up to the edge on the longer sides but leaving a $^1/_2$-inch/1-cm gap along the shorter sides. Spread a teaspoonful of Umeboshi paste along the bottom edge and on top of this place some of the bell pepper mixture and some of the fried tofu. Tuck in with the exposed edge of seaweed and roll up tightly like a jelly roll. Seal at the other end, moistening the edge with a drop of the marinade or water. Wrap each roll in plastic wrap and refrigerate (up to 2 days) before slicing into 8 pieces with a very sharp knife. Serve at once with the dipping sauce.

Pesto *and* Sun-dried Tomato Roulade

Roulades are surprisingly easy to make and look impressive as part of a cold buffet, sliced and arranged on a large platter. This roulade is especially attractive with its vibrant colors.

Serves 6–8

For the roulade
2 tbsp. butter, softened, for greasing paper
12 eggs, separated
2 tbsp. pesto
2 tbsp. sun-dried tomato paste (see page 11)
salt and pepper, to taste
For the filling
8 oz./200 g/1 cup low-fat cream cheese
1 tbsp. pine nuts, very lightly toasted
1 tbsp. finely chopped chives
2 roasted garlic cloves, skinned and puréed,
    or 2 garlic cloves, crushed

Heat the oven to 325°F/160°C. Line a 16 x 14-inch/40 x 35-cm cookie sheet with wax paper and grease generously with softened butter.

Place half the egg yolks in one bowl and the rest of the yolks in another bowl. Add pesto to one bowl and sun-dried tomato paste to the other. Season with salt and pepper and mix well. Whisk the egg whites until stiff and divide equally between the two bowls. Fold in gently with a metal spoon (a wooden spoon will flatten the egg white) until well incorporated.

Spread one half of the mixture along the length and halfway across the tray, then add the second mixture so you end up with two long parallel strips of filling. Bake in the oven for exactly 14 minutes until set.

Allow to cool for a few minutes and transfer to a second tray lined with overlapping plastic wrap. Let cool.

Mix all the filling ingredients together, then carefully spread over the roulade with a palette knife leaving a little gap around the edges so the filling does not spread out everywhere. Take care not to tear the roulade. Roll up gently like a jelly roll.

To serve, trim both ends to reveal all three colors.

If not using immediately, roll the roulade tightly like a jelly roll. Wrapped in plastic wrap it can be kept (unfilled) in the refrigerator for a day or two at the most. Add the filling shortly before serving.

Fennel *and* Ricotta Terrine *with an* Orange *and* Brandy Sauce

Orange and fennel make a successful marriage and here they are combined to make a lovely terrine. The mixture is rich and delectable and a small slice laced with orange and brandy sauce is quite heavenly!

1½ lb./700 g/4 cups fennel bulb, trimmed and cut into quarters **Serves 6–8**
2½ cups/600 ml water
¼ cup/60 ml olive oil
4 garlic cloves, finely sliced
1 tsp. bouillon powder
salt and pepper, to taste
6 eggs
1 lb./450 g/2 cups ricotta cheese
¼ cup/60 ml heavy cream
1 tbsp. finely chopped fresh chervil leaves
grated rind (zest) of 1 orange
chervil sprigs, to garnish
For the sauce
2 large oranges
just over 2 tbsp. unsalted butter
1 tsp. light brown sugar
½ cup/120 ml brandy

Heat the oven to 375°F/190°C. Place the fennel in a heavy-based pan together with the water, olive oil, garlic, bouillon powder, and salt and pepper. Cover and braise for about 10 minutes until the fennel is soft but not falling apart.

Place in a food processor or blender with the eggs, ricotta, and cream. Blend for a few seconds so there remains a little texture to the fennel. Add half the chopped chervil leaves, orange rind (zest), and a little more pepper.

Line a 1-lb./450-g loaf pan with wax paper and butter lightly. Pour in the mixture, cover with a piece of buttered wax paper, and place in a roasting pan containing a shallow layer of water. Bake in the oven for 1 hour until firm but not hard to the touch. Allow to cool before turning out.

To make the sauce, remove the rind (zest) from both oranges using a lemon zester and set aside. Squeeze the juice from one orange; remove the pith from the other orange and cut into slices. Place the butter and sugar in a small heavy-based saucepan and cover with the juice of one of the oranges. Heat very gently for a few minutes, then add the remaining orange slices and the brandy and cook gently for an additional 2 minutes.

To serve, turn out the terrine, pour the sauce over, and garnish with the remaining sprigs of fresh chervil.

Lemoned Carrot *and* Celeriac Terrine *with* Black Olives *in* Nori Seaweed

In this stunning terrine, glossy black seaweed encases layers of rich, creamy cheese and vegetables. Served sliced and topped with a luscious avocado sauce, it makes a truly glamorous starter.

Serves 6–8

3 sheets black nori seaweed

1½ lb./700 g/3½ cups celeriac, peeled and finely shredded

8 oz./225 g/1 cup mascarpone cheese

4 oz./100 g/½ cup low-fat cream cheese

1 tbsp. green Nori flakes, or finely chopped parsley

1 garlic clove, crushed

juice of ½ lemon

salt and pepper, to taste

8 oz./225 g/1½ cups black olives, pitted

1½ lb./700 g/3½ cups medium carrots,
   peeled and finely shredded

For the sauce

1 large, ripe avocado

4 tbsp. water

1 garlic clove, finely crushed

salt and pepper, to taste

Line a 1-lb./450-g loaf pan with plastic wrap and then with 2 sheets of nori seaweed. Mix the grated celeriac with the mascarpone and 2 oz./50 g/¼ cup cream cheese, then add the nori flakes or parsley, the crushed garlic, half of the lemon juice, and salt and pepper to taste.

Spread half of this mixture into the lined pan, pressing it down well with the back of a spoon. Add a layer of pitted black olives and press down, but not so much that they sink into the mixture.

Add the rest of the lemon to the carrots, and squeeze thoroughly to remove excess liquid. Add the remaining cream cheese and a little salt and pepper, mix thoroughly and spread on top of the olive layer.

Finally finish off with the remaining celeriac mixture. Press down and cover with the remaining sheet of seaweed, trimmed to size. Refrigerate for at least 1 hour.

To make the sauce, blend all ingredients together to a pouring consistency.

To serve, slice with an electric knife if possible or otherwise use a fine serrated knife.

Eggplant *and* Sun-dried Tomato Mousse *with a* Tomato *and* Yellow Bell Pepper Salad

An easy summer appetizer with a filling deliberately kept light with fromage frais to offset the inevitable richness of the fried eggplants. The eggplants have to be dark gold in color—do not compromise on this.

1½ large eggplants, cut into approximately 24 slices
salt and pepper, to taste
5 tbsp. olive oil
few drops Tabasco sauce
few drops balsamic vinegar
For the salad
12 oz./350 g/2½ cups firm deep-red tomatoes (about 3 medium) deseeded and cut into small even dice
1 yellow bell pepper, about 5 oz./125 g/1¼ cups, deseeded and cut into small even dice
½ cup/120 ml light and fruity olive oil
1 tbsp. balsamic vinegar
12 black olives, pitted and roughly torn into quarters
5 sprigs fresh coriander, stalks removed
salt and pepper, to taste

Serves 6

For the mousse
3 oz./75 g/¾ cup sun-dried tomato paste (see page 11) or a very good, bright red ready-made one
6 oz./175 g/¾ cup virtually fat-free fromage frais
1 tsp. hot water

Sprinkle the eggplant slices lightly with salt and set aside for about 1 hour to draw out any bitter juices. Rinse and pat dry.

Meanwhile, prepare the mousse by mixing the sun-dried tomato paste with the fromage frais and the hot water, which helps the amalgamation of the two. Place in a food processor and blend for about 30 seconds until light and smooth.

Heat the oil in a skillet until very hot, drop in 5–6 eggplant slices and fry until they are dark golden in color. Place on paper towels and immediately sprinkle with salt and a few drops of Tabasco and balsamic vinegar. Repeat with the remaining eggplant slices.

To assemble, place a large slice of eggplant on each individual plate and spread 1 tbsp. mousse over the top. Repeat this layering process once more and top with a third eggplant slice.

To make the salad garnish, mix the diced tomato with the yellow bell pepper. Mix together the olive oil, vinegar, and Tabasco, season with salt and pepper, and add into the salad. Spoon the salad generously around each eggplant mound. Garnish with olive quarters and coriander leaves and serve at once.

Following pages: Eggplant and Sun-dried Tomato Mousse with a Tomato and Yellow Bell Pepper Salad

Vegetable Tempura

Serve these deep-fried vegetables with aperitifs, as a starter with a dipping sauce of tamari, Tabasco, garlic, and ginger or, as the Japanese do, over miso soup for a delicious one-bowl meal. The batter can be made in advance without the addition of the egg white. This can be added just before use.

Serves 8–10

For the batter
just under 1 cup all-purpose flour
⅞ cup/200 ml lukewarm water
¼ cup/60 ml lager
salt and pepper, to taste
2 egg whites

For the vegetables
4 oz./100 g/¾ cup carrots, cut on the slant
1 small/2 cups cauliflower, cut into small flowerets
6 oz./175 g/2 cups broccoli, cut into small flowerets
4 oz./100 g/1¼ cups green beans
1 bunch scallions, green parts reserved for garnishing
1 qt./1 lt sunflower oil, for deep frying
4 oz./100 g/¾ cup zucchini, cut on the slant
4 oz./100 g/½ cup button mushrooms, left whole
4 oz./100 g/1 cup snow peas, trimmed
4 oz./100 g/1 cup onion, sliced into thin rings
1 red bell pepper,
    deseeded and cut into 2-inch/4-cm squares
1 yellow bell pepper,
    deseeded and cut into 2-inch/4-cm squares
4 oz./100 g/4 cups baby spinach
1 lb./450 g/4 cups firm plain tofu, drained of all liquid,
    cut into 1-inch/2-cm cubes and marinated (see pages 102–3)

Lightly blanch the carrots, cauliflower, broccoli, and green beans ready for cooking. Blanch the green parts of the scallions, press flat, and reserve for garnishing.

To make the batter, place all the ingredients except for the egg whites in a bowl and fold together gently with a wooden spoon. This prevents the batter from becoming elastic—an elastic batter will not coat well. Whisk the egg whites until they stand in soft peaks and fold into the batter immediately before use.

Heat the oil in a large saucepan or a deep-fat fryer until very hot. Dip a batch of vegetables and tofu into the batter to coat well. The batter should be thin enough to run off the vegetables in big drops. Carefully drop the coated food into the hot oil and cook until risen to the top and fried to a pale golden color. Remove at once to a colander or sieve lined with several layers of paper towels. Sprinkle with salt while piping hot. Coat and fry the remaining vegetables in the same way.

Wrap the blanched scallion strips around the tofu cubes, holding them in place with wooden toothpicks if necessary. Serve immediately.

Almond *and* Tofu Cigars *with* Green Olive Confit

Filo cigars with fillings of every kind, savory and sweet, are as common to Moroccan cooking as sandwiches are to English cooking, but about a hundred times more delicate. The green olive confit is more usually associated with chicken and is full-bodied enough for the mild filling. As ever, the search for a balance of taste leads to a simple if unexpected combination. I hesitate to say so, but the more traditional filling would have been brains! Filo cigars are usually served as one of several predinner nibbles or in neat pyramid piles at feasts and wedding banquets.

Makes about 20 cigars

14 sheets filo pastry, about 14 x 8 inches/35 x 20 cm in size
3 cups/750 ml sunflower oil for deep frying
fine strips of lemon rind (zest) and coriander sprigs, to garnish
For the filling
1 lb./450 g/4 cups firm plain tofu
2 tsp. bouillon powder
1 cup/230 ml water
1 large onion, finely chopped
1 pinch grated nutmeg
salt and pepper, to taste
1 whole egg yolk
1 hard-boiled egg, finely chopped
2 oz./50 g/¹/₃ cup almonds, lightly roasted in their skins,
    roughly chopped
1 tbsp. finely chopped fresh coriander or parsley
For the confit
1 large onion, finely sliced
3 garlic cloves
2 tbsp. olive oil
¹/₂ cup/120 ml stock, made with ¹/₂ tsp. bouillon powder
8 oz./225 g/just over 1¹/₂ cups pitted green olives
juice of 1 lemon

To make the filling, roughly break up the tofu into a bowl and cover with the bouillon powder dissolved in the water. Allow to marinate for at least 2 hours or even overnight if possible. Strain, reserving the liquid.

Fry the onion in a little of the oil until a dark golden brown. A pale onion will not give the same results. Add the strained tofu, nutmeg, and salt and pepper and continue to fry for 5–10 minutes over a fairly high heat, turning constantly but allowing the tofu to stick to the pan a little so it begins to brown in places. Add a little of the reserved stock only if the mixture begins to look too dry. Remove from the heat and quickly stir in the egg yolk. Add the finely chopped hard-boiled egg, the almonds, and coriander or parsley and set aside to cool.

To make the cigars, take 2 sheets of pastry, place one on top of the other and cut into 3 equal-sized strips. Place a little of the filling at one end of each strip, leaving $1/2$-inch/1-cm gap on either side. Fold these edges in and tightly roll up the pastry, sealing the ends with a little water. Repeat until all the mixture is used up.

Heat the sunflower oil in a deep saucepan or deep-fat fryer until very hot. Gently drop in 3–4 cigars and fry until they are golden brown. Transfer to a colander lined with paper towel and allow to drain.

To make the sauce, fry the onion and garlic in the oil until golden brown. Season with salt and pepper, add the stock and simmer gently for a few minutes. Add the green olives and continue to simmer for 5 minutes only. Add the lemon juice and remove from the heat.

Garnish the cigars with fine strips of lemon rind (zest) and a few sprigs of fresh coriander or parsley and serve with the sauce.

Lemon Rice *with* Julienne *of* Carrot *and* Zucchini

This makes a great accompaniment to all kinds of roasted, broiled, or stir-fried vegetables.

Serves 6

For the rice

8 oz./225 g/1 cup short-grain, organic brown rice

4 oz./100 g/¹/₂ cup wild rice

4–5 saffron strands
   infused in ¹/₄ cup/60 ml hot water for 30 minutes

dash of olive oil

8 oz./225 g/1¹/₂ cups carrots, cut into thin matchstick strips

salt and pepper, to taste

8 oz./225 g/1¹/₂ cups zucchini,
   cut into thin matchstick strips

juice and rind (zest) of 1 lemon

Tabasco to taste

1 tbsp. sesame seeds

2 tbsp. chopped fresh parsley

For the garnish

8 oz./225 g/1¹/₂ cups carrots

8 oz./225 g/1¹/₂ cups zucchini

Cook the rice (in 1¹/₂ times water to rice), with the saffron liquid if using, for about 45 minutes with a heavy lid on.

Heat oil in a skillet and stir-fry the carrots for about 30–40 seconds. Add a little salt and pepper. Cook the zucchini in the same way for about 20 seconds—do not add more oil. Remove the vegetables from the skillet and quickly stir into the drained rice. Pour the lemon juice, Tabasco, half the sesame seeds, half the lemon rind (zest), and half the parsley over the vegetable mixture. Mix well. For the garnish, peel the carrots and zucchini, then shave into thin ribbons using a vegetable peeler. Cook the carrot ribbons in the skillet, without extra oil, for 1 minute, adding the zucchini after 30 seconds. Season lightly with salt and pepper, then stir in the rest of the sesame seeds.

Heap the rice onto a serving plate and place the ribbons on top. Sprinkle with the rest of the parsley and lemon rind (zest) and serve.

Leek *and* Almond Terrine

Weighting down the terrine is the most crucial part of the recipe. It ensures that the leeks hold together, making slicing easier.

20 young leeks, trimmed to an even size   Serves 6
¼ cup/60 ml olive oil
2½ cups/600 ml water for braising
½ tsp. bouillon powder
1 garlic clove, crushed
1 tsp. agar flakes
salt and pepper, to taste
4 oz./100 g/1 cup toasted slivered almonds
For the dressing
1 tsp. grain mustard
4 tbsp. white wine vinegar
½ cup/120 ml olive oil
1 garlic clove, crushed
1 tbsp. chopped chives

Trim the leeks and make a slit one layer deep. Remove this outer layer and reserve. Wash the leeks and place in a saucepan with the oil, water, bouillon, and crushed garlic. Cook gently for 5 minutes. Remove from the heat and reserve. Gently braise the reserved outer layers in a little oil for about a minute until wilted and just tender. Set aside.

Line a 1-lb./450-g loaf pan with plastic wrap and then with the leek outer layers, holding each at a right angle to the pan and draping them over, leaving half of each leaf to overhang. Remove the leeks from the liquid in the saucepan and pack tightly into the loaf pan. Reduce the liquid over high heat to about half, dissolve the agar flakes in a little of the hot liquid and return to the pan. Continue to reduce for another minute, then add salt and pepper and pour over the leeks.

Weight the terrine by placing several packs of butter, or a package of frozen peas, or any heavy object, on top. Refrigerate for several hours before turning out.

To make the dressing, dissolve the grain mustard in the vinegar and slowly beat in the olive oil. Finally, add the garlic and the finely chopped chives and season with salt and pepper.

Before serving, sprinkle with the toasted almond slivers so they adhere to the top and to all sides.

Following pages: Mushroom Parfait with Apricot and Onion Confit served with Vegetable Chips

Mushroom Parfait *with* Apricot *and* Onion Confit

This started life as my very first vegetarian creation, twelve years ago. I will never forget the moment, the miniscule airless kitchen and the friend standing in the doorway, pronouncing it perfect. As a Paté de Champignons en Croute it contained many more nuts (just as finely puréed) and was encased in a puff pastry braid. It was the single most requested item on my menu and I once went into production hoping to make my fortune on it. However, for this book, I wanted to modernize the recipe and at the eleventh hour I suddenly came up with the idea of the apricot and onion confit and the lighter mousse-like parfait, which I always serve with the ever-so-thin Vegetable Chips (see page 55). But treat this dish with reverence; it is extremely rich for all its lightness. Eat it with a mixed salad of strong leaves, such as radiccio, Belgian endive and the young part of a curly endive. One parfait quenelle, served as an appetizer, is as much of a good thing as you will need.

Serves 8–10

¼ cup/60 ml sunflower oil

9 oz./275 g/2 cups onion, diced

1½ lb./700 g/9 cups chopped chestnut mushrooms

1 large sprig tarragon,
   with a few leaves reserved for garnish (optional)

3 garlic cloves, crushed

1 tbsp. tamari

1 piece star anise

3 tbsp. Marsala wine

3 oz./75 g/½ cup broken cashew pieces

¼ cup/60 ml water

2 oz./50 g/generous ½ cup ground almonds

1 tbsp. toasted fine breadcrumbs

1 cup/230 ml heavy cream, whipped

finely chopped and whole chives, to garnish

For the confit

1 lb./450 g/3 cups pearl onions

1½ cups/360 ml water

a scant ½ cup/100 ml sunflower oil

8–9 oz./250 g/1⅓ cup dried apricots

1 tbsp. light brown sugar

4–6 large ripe fresh apricots, halved

Heat the oil and fry the diced onion for 10 minutes until soft and brown. Wash the mushrooms and add them to the pan. Lower the heat, add the whole sprig of tarragon, the crushed garlic, tamari, and star anise and cook for 5 minutes. Add the Marsala wine, cook for another 15 minutes, stirring at regular intervals. Remove the star anise and blend to a smooth purée. Set aside to cool completely.

Meanwhile, place the cashew nuts and water in a food processor and blend to a very smooth paste. Add this, the ground almonds, and the breadcrumbs to the mushroom mixture. Now whip the cream until soft peaks form and fold in. Refrigerate for at least 1 hour.

To make the confit, blanch the onions in boiling water for 1 minute. Drain, cool, and peel. Return to the pan, cover with the water and oil, and add the dried apricots and sugar. Cover with a lid and simmer for at least 30 minutes, checking that the water does not evaporate before the onion is soft and caramelized. You may need to add a little extra water. If, after 20 minutes, the onion is still very white and there is still a substantial amount of liquid left, bring to a fierce boil for a couple of minutes, until it begins to brown, then lower the heat once more. Add the fresh apricots toward the end of cooking time. Some of the apricot should dissolve to give a pale orange-colored sauce, thin enough to pour. Again, add a little water if necessary.

To serve, form the parfait into quenelles, pressing them into shape between two tablespoons. Place a quenelle in the center of each serving plate, then pour some of the confit around each quenelle. Arrange 2 pearl onions and 3 apricots on each plate. Garnish with the whole and chopped chives, scattering the chopped chives over the quenelles. Scatter 2–3 tarragon leaves over the confit on each serving if using. Scatter with *Vegetable Chips* (see page 55) and serve.

Chive *and* Parmesan Sable *with* Two Fillings *and* a Sauce

There is only one way to eat pastry and that is when it is as light as a whisper, as thin as a sheet, and as melting as the butter it is made with. The fragility of this delicate appetizer pleads for it to be assembled at the last possible moment. Let your guests wait and expect to see their faces break into smiles of pure pleasure as the pastry melts in their mouths.

Serves 6

3^1/$_5$ cups all-purpose white flour

1 tsp. salt

2^1/$_4$ sticks unsalted butter

3 tbsp. water

1 oz./25 g/^{1}/$_4$ cup freshly grated Parmesan cheese

1 garlic clove, crushed

juice and rind (zest) of 1 lemon

For the artichoke and green olives filling

6 fresh, cooked artichoke hearts (see page 59), chopped into dice

6 oz./175 g/1^1/$_5$ cups lemon-stuffed green olives, or plain green olives
    pitted, roughly chopped

2 handfuls young arugula leaves, torn into pieces

^{1}/$_2$ tbsp. finely chopped chives

couple of dashes of Tabasco sauce

pepper, to taste

For the tomato, red onion, and basil filling

12 oz./350 g/2^1/$_2$ cups firm, red tomatoes,
    deseeded and chopped into small dice

3 oz./75 g/just over ^{1}/$_2$ cup red onion, finely diced

1 large basil leaf, finely shredded

For the sauce

1^1/$_2$ cups/360 ml plain yogurt, smetana,
    or a mixture of the two

1^1/$_2$ tsp. sun-dried tomato paste (see page 11)

1 tbsp. water

Sift the flour into a mixing bowl, together with the salt. Cut the cold butter into small cubes, add to the flour and lightly rub in with the tips of your fingers. (Make sure your hands are cold—hold them under very cold water, if necessary.) With light movements turn the butter and flour, together with the Parmesan and garlic, into light, fine crumbs. Then add the cold water and lemon juice and, using one hand, lightly bind together to form a dough. Wrap in plastic wrap and refrigerate for 30 minutes.

Heat the oven to 400°F/200°C. Make sure that your surface is adequately floured, then roll out the pastry very thinly, almost as if it were pasta. With your fingers tear a series of rough circles about 4 inches/10 cm in diameter. (You will need about 18 but make a few extra since they are so delicate that they are liable to break.) Place them in batches of two or three, depending on your oven space, on lightly floured cookie sheets.

Bake for 10 minutes until crisp and just lightly beginning to bubble. Remove from the trays and allow to cool, preferably on cooling racks.

Meanwhile, make the fillings and sauce. To make the artichoke and green olive filling, mix the artichokes with the olives, arugula, and finely chopped chives. Season with Tabasco and black pepper. (Note that you do not need to add salt because of the saltiness of the olives.) Set aside. To make the tomato filling, mix the ingredients together and season with salt and pepper. Set aside. To make the sauce, mix the yogurt with the tomato paste and water.

To assemble, place a pastry round on each plate, then spoon on one filling. Lightly drizzle a spoonful of the sauce over each, then top with a second pastry round. Spoon on the second filling, top with a little more sauce and finish with a third pastry round. Use any remaining sauce to drizzle around the outside and scatter a little of each filling around the plate. Serve immediately.

Olive Focaccia

You could happily substitute the thyme and oregano with the same amount of basil or a mixture of basil and marjoram, both of which are milder and sweeter.

Serves 8

7 cups all-purpose flour

pinch of salt

1 tsp. sugar

1½ cups/360 ml warm water

2 tbsp. dried yeast

½ cup/120 ml olive oil, plus extra for oiling

½ cup/120 ml dry white wine

14 oz./400 g/1 generous cup pitted black olives, roughly chopped

1 tbsp. chopped fresh thyme

2 tbsp. chopped fresh oregano

coarse sea salt, for sprinkling

Put the flour and salt in a mixing bowl and make a well in the center. Dissolve the sugar in 1 cup warm water. Sprinkle in the dried yeast and whisk well. Cover the liquid with plastic wrap and stand in a warm, draft-free place for about 10–15 minutes until frothy. Pour into the well.

Stir in the olive oil and wine, then add the rest of the warm water. Work the dough until it holds together in a ball. Knead well for 10–15 minutes until soft and elastic and a small depression made with your finger springs back when you release the pressure. You may need to add a little extra flour if it becomes too sticky.

Mix in three-quarters of the black olives. Mix the herbs together and knead in one-third. Place in a mixing bowl, cover with a damp cloth, and leave to rise for about 1½ hours, or until it has doubled in size.

Heat the oven to 425°F/220°C. Knock back the dough for a couple of minutes. Then roll out on a floured surface to a ½-inch/1-cm thickness.

Place the dough on an oiled cookie sheet and spread out with your hands. Sprinkle the coarse sea salt and the remaining olives and herbs on top. Press down into the dough with your fingers to make several deep crevices.

Bake in the oven for 20 minutes or until the focaccia is golden in color. Brush with the extra olive oil and serve hot.

Vegetable Chips

These ever-so-thin vegetable chips are perfect as snack or starter and an ideal accompaniment to **Mushroom Parfait with Apricot and Onion Confit** *(see pages 50–1). You can also use parsnips and sweet potatoes in the same way.*

1 lb./450 g potatoes, cut into very thin slices   Serves 8–10
1 lb./450 g raw beets, cut into very thin slices
sunflower oil, for deep frying
salt, to taste

Pat dry the potato and beet slices with a cloth. Heat the oil in a deep saucepan or deep-fat fryer, drop a batch of slices into the oil and fry until golden and crisp. Immediately lay on paper towels and sprinkle with salt. Fry the remaining slices in the same way.

Following pages: Fennel and Walnut Salad with Raspberries

Salads & Vegetables

Warm Asparagus *and* Pan-fried Potato Salad *with* Baby Spinach

Simply be careful, when making this recipe, not to burn the tamari or the balsamic vinegar. If you see a danger of this, quickly add a few drops of water to the pan and lower the heat. Use the smallest potatoes you can find and the finest asparagus tips.

Serves 6
salt, for boiling
1½ lb./750 g/2 cups thin-stemmed asparagus, trimmed
1 red bell pepper
12 oz./350 g/2 cups small new potatoes
3 tbsp. olive oil
1 large red onion, cut into large chunks
6 tbsp. balsamic vinegar
3 tbsp. Cognac
1 tbsp. tamari
3 garlic cloves, crushed
1½ lb./750 g/2 cups baby spinach

Bring a pan of salted water to a boil and plunge in the asparagus tips for no more than 3 minutes so they remain al dente and can bear a further couple of minutes of cooking later on. Drain immediately.

Broil the red bell pepper until charred on all sides, then peel, deseed, and cut into even slivers. Fry in a dry skillet for a few seconds until they begin to char slightly; remove from the pan and set aside.

Place the potatoes in a pan of cold salted water, bring to a boil and cook for about 15–20 minutes or until tender. Drain, run under cold water, and cut all but the very smallest potatoes in half. Heat half the olive oil and quickly sauté the red onion so that it retains its color and texture. Set aside. Heat the rest of the olive oil and add the potatoes. Fry until they are golden and crisp on the outside.

Add the vinegar, brandy, tamari, and crushed garlic and sauté over a brisk heat but without allowing the juices to evaporate. (Add a little water if necessary.) Then remove from the heat, add the spinach so that it wilts in the heat of the potatoes. Finally, add the onion and asparagus to the pan. Toss quickly. Add the slivers of red bell pepper and serve immediately.

Arugula *and* Artichoke Salad *with* Paen Careg Cheese *and a* Walnut Vinaigrette

Paen Careg is an organic vegetarian cheese. Use a ripe goats' cheese if you are unable to find it. Baby artichokes with long stems, freshly cooked and cut into quarters, also look lovely in this salad. Make sure your arugula is fresh and crisp.

6 small globe artichokes or
1 lb./450 g/5 cups canned artichoke hearts
1 lemon, plus a squeeze of lemon juice (for fresh artichokes)
1½ tsp. grain mustard
2 garlic cloves, finely chopped
2 tbsp. balsamic vinegar
salt and pepper, to taste
4 tbsp. walnut oil
9 oz./275 g/4½ cups arugula
2 oz./50 g/½ cup roughly chopped walnuts
6 oz./175 g/2 cups Paen Careg cheese, thinly sliced

Serves 6

To prepare fresh artichokes, cut off the stems, remove the tough outer leaves, and slice the rest of the leaves to just above the choke. Bring a large saucepan of water to a boil together with the juice of 1 lemon, and cook the artichoke hearts for about 20 minutes. Refresh immediately in a bowl of iced water and pull out the fibrous choke. Squeeze a little lemon juice over to prevent the hearts from turning black. For canned artichoke hearts, rinse and drain.

Make a simple dressing by mixing the mustard, garlic, vinegar, and salt and pepper, and whisking in the oil.

Place the artichokes in a dish, pour the dressing over, and allow to marinate for as long as you can (preferably for at least 1 hour). Rinse and pat dry the arugula leaves, taking care not to bruise them. Just before serving, toss the leaves into the dressing for the briefest moment and garnish with the chopped walnuts and sliced cheese. Serve at once.

Orange *and* Black-Olive Salad

Use Greek or French Provençale black olives. You could also mix green and black olives together. Without the orange, this is a perfect predinner accompaniment to cold drinks, especially cold beer. One mouthful and you can just imagine the sea and the salt air.

Serves 6
3 large oranges
8 oz./225 g/1⅓ cups black olives, washed and pitted
2 garlic cloves
1 tsp. cumin
1 tsp. sweet paprika
  (or half paprika, half chili powder depending on your taste)
3 tbsp. olive oil
dash of Tabasco sauce
pinch of salt

Peel the oranges, removing all the pith. Cut into small even-size pieces and mix with the olives.

Chop the garlic finely with a knife (don't crush it because it becomes too messy). Mix with the cumin, paprika, oil, Tabasco, and salt. Stir into the oranges and olives and serve at once or set aside for 1–2 hours. Serve with cold drinks and chunks of white bread to mop up the delicious sauce.

Beet Salad *with* Cumin *and* Red Onion

I prefer very simple salads and none more than this ancient Moroccan one. I loved it even as a child and used to enjoy painting my lips red with the beet. Serve it on a bed of fresh, crisp watercress for a piquant and contemporary touch. The longer you can leave the beets to marinate the better—overnight is ideal.

1 lb./450 g/1¹/₂ cups raw beets   Serves 6
salt, for boiling
1 oz./25 g/¹/₅ cup red onion, finely diced
2 tsp. cider vinegar
1 tsp. sunflower oil
1 heaped tsp. cumin powder
1 tsp. Tabasco
1 heaped tsp. chopped fresh parsley, to garnish
8 oz./225 g/3 cups watercress

Cook the beets in boiling salted water for about 1¹/₂ hours until soft. Drain, reserving ¹/₄ cup/60 ml of the cooking liquid. Allow the beets to cool, then peel and cut into ¹/₄-inch/5-mm slices.

Place the beet slices in a dish, add the reserved cooking liquid and half the onion, the vinegar, oil, cumin, and Tabasco. Let marinate for 1 hour at room temperature.

Drain and garnish with the parsley and remaining onion and serve on a bed of watercress. The flavors improve on keeping so this salad is even better the next day.

Fennel *and* Walnut Salad
with Raspberries

The saltiness of the olives, the depth of the walnut oil, and the sharp tanginess of orange juice and raspberries combine brilliantly with the fresh, sweet taste of fennel. Fresh young walnuts, with skins that peel off to reveal the purest white flesh, are a passing treat to make the most of in this salad. Use a moist and gentle goats' cheese. If you can use small young bulbs of fennel so much the better, for this salad is an "Ode to Youth Culture."

Serves 6

1 lb./450 g/3 medium or 6 small fennel bulbs

1 oak leaf lettuce, with the older darker leaves removed

2 oz./50 g/¼ cup black olives

3 oz./75 g/½ cup raspberries

2 oz./50 g or 3 small goats' cheeses, cut into portions

¾ cup/180 ml freshly squeezed orange juice

¼ cup/60 ml walnut oil

dash of Tabasco sauce

salt and pepper, to taste

6 shelled fresh walnuts,
   with as much of the skins removed as possible and sliced

Chop off the tough ends from the fennel and cut into paper-thin slices; reserve the feathery leaves for garnishing. Place in a bowl together with the separated leaves from the oak leaf lettuce. Add the black olives, half the raspberries, and goats' cheese.

Blend the orange juice with the remaining raspberries, walnut oil, Tabasco, and salt and pepper to taste. Pour over the salad and garnish with the fennel leaves and sliced walnuts.

Cherry Tomato, Black Olive, *and* Quail Egg Salad *with a* Cream *and* Lemon Dressing

This has to be one of the prettiest salads, made as it is with miniature pop-in-the-mouth ingredients.

12 oz./350 g/1 medium head broccoli
iced water
½ cup/120 ml light cream
juice of ½ lemon
1 tbsp. mayonnaise
2 garlic cloves, crushed
1 tsp. grain mustard
salt and pepper, to taste
12 quail eggs
12 oz./350 g/2 cups cherry tomatoes
2 oz./50 g/⅓ cup black olives

Serves 6

Place the broccoli head in a saucepan of salted water and blanch for no more than 2 minutes, so the broccoli is bright green and just tender. Refresh immediately in a prepared bowl of iced water or simply under a cold running faucet. Break into small even-sized flowerets, trimming off the stem. Peel off the tough outer skin of the stem and cut it into even-sized matchstick strips.

Mix the light cream, lemon juice, mayonnaise, garlic, mustard, and salt and pepper together to make the dressing.

Boil the quail eggs for 2½ minutes and peel them with care. Cut in half.

Mix the broccoli with the tomatoes and black olives, stir in the dressing, then add the quail eggs. Serve at once while the broccoli and eggs are still warm. If serving cold, add the broccoli at the last minute or it will be discolored by the lemon juice.

Spinach *and* Avocado Salad *with* Pumpkin Seeds *and* Dried Mango

Be sure to use a moist and succulent-looking dried mango and not the tough and dull looking specimens sometimes on sale.

Serves 6
2 oz./50 g/¹/₂ cup pumpkin seeds
1 ripe but firm avocado
¹/₂ lemon
4 oz./100 g/1¹/₄ cups Caerphilly cheese, roughly broken up
1¹/₄ lb./500 g/7 cups baby spinach
2 oz./50 g/¹/₂ cup dried mango slices, cut into thin slithers or left whole
For the dressing
2 tbsp. olive oil
1 tbsp. tamari
1 tbsp. water
2 drops Tabasco sauce

Lightly fry the pumpkin seeds in a dry skillet with a little salt. Peel the avocado and cut into slivers; squeeze the lemon juice over the avocado to prevent discoloration. Toss the avocado with the Caerphilly, spinach, mango slices, and pumpkin seeds in a large bowl. Whisk the dressing ingredients together and add at the very last minute. Arrange the salad on a large plate or platter, exposing as much of the mango and avocado as possible.

Belgian Endive *and* Blueberry Salad *with a* Dolcelatte Dressing

Thank you to my friend Jack, who suggested the blueberries in this salad as we walked around the supermarket searching for ingredients and inspiration. Belgian endive with its bitterness can take the power of Dolcelatte, and the blueberries add a delicious sweetening balance.

1 lb./450 g/2 large heads Belgian endive   Serves 6
3 tbsp. smetana or sour cream
4 oz./100 g/1 cup Dolcelatte
2 tbsp. water
4 oz./100 g/½ cup blueberries
3 walnut halves, finely sliced
freshly ground black pepper, to taste

Trim the Belgian endive, removing any brown parts and separating the leaves. Place on a large plate in a random fashion. With a fork or hand-held electric blender, blend together the Dolcelatte, smetana, and water and pour all over the leaves. Scatter the blueberries and finally the walnut slices over the entire salad. Season with the black pepper and serve at once.

Melon *and* Avocado Salad *with* Brie *in a* Smetana Dressing

Many years ago, I ran the kitchen of a 170-seater vegetarian restaurant in Zurich. It was way ahead of its time and I believe it is still going to this day. This was one of its delicious salads and can be served as an appetizer. But it must be made at the last minute and served very fresh. Do not add salt, which would make the melon weep uncontrollably and spoil the delicate balance of flavors.

Serves 6
1 Cantaloupe melon
1 Honeydew melon
1 large ripe avocado
4 oz./100 g/1 cup brie cut into ½-inch/1-cm cubes
2 tbsp. smetana or sour cream
1 small, young curly endive lettuce,
    pale yellow inner leaves only
freshly ground black pepper, to taste

Use a melon baller to scoop out the flesh from both melons and the avocado. Place in a large bowl, add the bie and smetana and mix lightly.

Serve on individual plates on a bed of curly endive lettuce. Sprinkle with freshly ground black pepper and serve immediately.

Pasta *and* Wild Mushroom Salad *with* Pistachios

You could use any combination of wild mushrooms, including dried ones, which often have the strongest and most distinctive flavor of all. But try having at least three different varieties. The touch of sugar simply rounds off the taste.

1 lb./450 g/3$\frac{1}{2}$ cups orechiette pasta or another twisted pasta   **Serves 6**
4 oz./100 g/2 cups girolle mushrooms
4 oz./100 g/2 cups chanterelle mushrooms
4 oz./100 g/2 cups oyster mushrooms
$\frac{1}{2}$ cup/120 ml fruity olive oil
1 tbsp. brandy
1 tbsp. tamari
1 tbsp. balsamic vinegar
$\frac{1}{2}$ tsp. light brown sugar
2 garlic cloves, finely chopped
2 oz./50 g/$\frac{1}{2}$ cup pistachio nuts
$\frac{1}{2}$ oz./15 g/$\frac{1}{4}$ cup fresh basil
$\frac{1}{2}$ oz./15 g/$\frac{1}{4}$ cup fresh tarragon (optional)
salt and pepper, to taste
dash of light cream (optional)

Bring the pasta to a boil in plenty of salted boiling water, drain and refresh immediately under cold running water. Set aside.

Meanwhile, rinse the mushrooms very carefully, taking care not to bruise them; tear the oyster mushrooms into large pieces or leave whole if they are already small and remove any tough ends.

Heat half the olive oil, reduce the heat and immediately add in the brandy, tamari, balsamic vinegar, sugar, and garlic, making sure that the garlic does not burn and that the other ingredients do not evaporate. (Should this happen, loosen the juices with a drop of water.)

Add the mushrooms at once, leaving the oyster mushrooms until last. Toss for no more than a couple of minutes, so that the mushrooms keep their shape but are cooked right through. Mix with the pasta and the remaining olive oil.

Chop two-thirds of the pistachios and two-thirds of the basil quite finely, either with a very sharp knife or in a pestle and mortar. Mix into the pasta salad together with the remaining nuts, basil, and tarragon, if using. Season with salt and pepper to taste.

Garnish with a few fresh basil leaves and pistachios, making sure the mushrooms show through. This salad improves on resting for a couple of hours and is best served at room temperature. It can be eaten hot with or without an additional dash of light cream.

Following pages: Pasta and Wild Mushroom Salad with Pistachios

White Cabbage Salad *with* Nori Flakes *and* Sesame Seeds

I usually serve this as part of a mixed salad platter, for an all-raw food lunch.

Serves 6   1 small head white cabbage, about 1 lb./450 g
2 heaped tbsp. sesame seeds
1 heaped tbsp. nori seaweed flakes
grated rind of 1 orange
juice of ½ orange (optional)
1 tbsp. tamari
1 tsp. sesame seed oil
1 tbsp. mayonnaise
salt, to taste
Tabasco sauce, to taste
1 sheet black nori seaweed, roughly torn, to garnish

Shred or shave the cabbage as finely as possible. Mix together all the other ingredients, except for the black seaweed, and add to the cabbage. Set aside for about 1 hour to allow the flavors to develop. Garnish with the torn seaweed sheet.

Chick-pea Salad *with* Onion, Coriander, *and* Cumin

Another dish in the Moroccan vein, the dressing is especially rich and evocative of Arabic climes. Serve this with warm pita bread or, better still, large flat Arabic bread or Focaccia (see page 54).

½ cup/120 ml olive oil	Serves 6
½ tbsp. paprika	
½ tbsp. cumin	
8 oz./225 g/1⅓ cups potatoes	
salt, to taste	
dash of Tabasco sauce	
2 garlic cloves, crushed	
1 small bunch coriander, chopped	
1 tbsp. chopped fresh parsley	
4½ cups cooked chick-peas	
juice of ½ lemon	
1 onion, chopped into dice	
2 cups/460 ml plain yogurt	

Mix the olive oil with the paprika and cumin and leave to dissolve for at least 30 minutes. Cook the spice mixture in a small saucepan over a low heat, adding a little water if necessary, then set aside to cool.

Boil the potatoes in boiling salted water for 20 minutes or until tender. Drain and cut in 1-inch/2-cm-square chunks.

Mix the spice mixture with the Tabasco, crushed garlic, and half the herbs. Stir in the potatoes, chick-peas, lemon juice, and onion.

Either mix in the yogurt or serve it separately, a spoonful for each person. Garnish with the remaining herbs.

Following pages: Warm Beet Salad with Pears and an Olive Salsa

Warm Beet Salad *with* Pears *and an* Olive Salsa

This exquisite combination of flavors came to me in the middle of the night!

Serves 6

8 oz./225 g/²/₃ cup beets
salt, for boiling
3 ripe pears
¹/₂ tsp. ginger powder
2 tbsp. butter
Tabasco sauce, to taste
1 tsp. balsamic vinegar
1 tsp. chopped fresh parsley
8 whole basil leaves
For the sauce
6 oz./175 g/1 cup mixed green and black olives
    (preferably Provençale), pitted and chopped
1 cup/230 ml Greek yogurt
1 tbsp. chopped fresh coriander
1 garlic clove, crushed
2 oz./50 g/¹/₂ cup pecan nuts,
    lightly toasted and roughly chopped

Cook the beets in salted boiling water for about 1¹/₂ hours until soft. Drain, reserving ¹/₄ cup/60 ml of the cooking liquid. Peel the beets and slice.

Cut the pears into quarters, remove the core, and slice.

Place the sliced beets together with the reserved cooking liquid and the ginger powder in a skillet and heat through for about 2 minutes. Add the butter and pears and cook for 2–3 minutes longer until the pears are well coated in the beet juice and are beginning to soften but are still firm. Add the Tabasco and balsamic vinegar and turn the heat off.

Meanwhile, make the sauce: Mix the chopped olives with the yogurt. Add the coriander, garlic, and pecan nuts.

Arrange the beets and pears on a large plate, sprinkle with parsley, and serve while still warm with the yogurt and olive sauce. Garnish with the basil leaves.

Braised Fennel

Braised vegetables, cooked slowly in a little oil, water, and usually garlic, are found all over the Mediterranean. No cries for al dente here. Vegetables are melt-in-the-mouth tender and cooked à l'étouffée with a heavy lid to conserve every particle of flavor. This treatment is given to celery, celeriac, salsify, carrots, green beans, even potatoes.

4 fennel bulbs, about 1½ lb./700 g/4 cups   Serves 4–6
1 tbsp. sunflower oil
3 garlic cloves, finely sliced
salt and pepper, to taste

Trim the tough green stalks from the fennel, reserving the fine feathery leaves. Cut the fennel into quarters and pack into a heavy-based pan, together with 1 cup/230 ml water, oil, garlic, and salt and pepper. Cover with a lid. Bring to a boil and simmer gently for about 20 minutes until soft.

Remove the lid and reduce any remaining liquid. There should be no water left at all and the fennel should have just begun to color slightly.

Serve with pasta or wild rice.

Braised Celery *with* Cream

If you can, use tender young hearts of celery, which are pale and almost sweet tasting. Celery is an excellent source of potassium—the salt we do need as opposed to the potentially harmful sodium we have mostly become addicted to.
Braised celery is delicious with buckwheat or organic short-grain brown rice, lightly sprinkled with Gomasio (another healthy way of eating salt, this time pounded with sesame seeds) and cream. It is also good with large flat ribbons of pasta.

3 celery stalks   Serves 6
3 garlic cloves, crushed
6 tbsp. heavy cream (optional)
salt and pepper, to taste

Wash the celery and remove any thick strings. Cut in half and place in a saucepan with the rest of the ingredients and $2^1/_2$ cups/600 ml water.

Bring to a boil, then simmer, covered, for 15 minutes over a low heat, topping up with a little extra water if the liquid begins to dry out. Remove the lid and continue to cook until all the liquid has evaporated and the celery is gently frying to a light golden brown.

Braised Salsify

The most unusual of root vegetables, salsify, has a black skin, which is always covered with earth. This calls upon another early childhood memory—we ate salsify in Morocco with the frequency usually reserved for potatoes and other prosaic fare. The preparation may be time consuming, but worth seeking out since you will be rewarded with a subtle and delicate flavor. Salsify can also be turned into soups or roasted like parsnips.

3 lemons   Serves 6
1 lb./450 g/2 cups salsify
1/4 cup/60 ml olive oil
2 garlic cloves, finely sliced
1 tsp. finely chopped fresh parsley

Halve 2 of the lemons and cut the remaining lemon into quarters.

Working as quickly as you can, scrape the barklike peel away from the salsify. Immediately rub each one with a lemon half and immerse in cold water acidulated with a little lemon juice to stop them from blackening.

Cut into manageable lengths and place in a saucepan with 1 cup/230 ml water, olive oil, garlic, and the lemon quarters. Bring to a boil and then simmer gently for 40–45 minutes until the water has evaporated and the salsify is quite soft and has fried to a pale golden brown on some of its sides. Dust with the very finely chopped parsley to serve.

Potatoes *in* Olive Oil *with* Turmeric *and* Saffron

A rich, intense combination that can serve as a great base for other vegetables, especially wild mushrooms. The potatoes should be waxy and tender.

Serves 6   3 lb./1.4 g/6 cups waxy potatoes
½ cup/120 ml olive oil
2 garlic cloves, finely sliced
a handful of fresh basil leaves
1 tsp. turmeric
1 tsp. saffron powder
salt and pepper, to taste

Heat the oven to 400°F/200°C. Peel the potatoes and cut into ⅛-inch/3-mm slices. Pat dry and mix with the olive oil, ¼ cup/60 ml water and the rest of the ingredients. Place in an ovenproof dish and cover tightly with a lid or foil.

Bake for 1 hour until the potatoes have softened and turned a lovely yellow color. Remove from the oven before they begin to turn brown or go crisp.

Serve this dish with a selection of braised vegetables. Alternatively, it works well arranged as a galette on a serving dish, topped with sautéed baby vegetables.

Mashed Potatoes

Winter would not be the same without mashed potato. In fact, thank goodness for cold days. My version of mashed potato is wonderfully indulgent—I like to add not only butter but also cream and olive oil. Wicked! Serve with the **Wild Mushroom Fricassee with Glazed Onions and Prune Confit** *(see page 110).*

2¼ lb./1 kg/6 cups potatoes   Serves 6
salt and pepper, to taste
5 tbsp. butter
½ cup/120 ml olive oil
2 tbsp. light cream
1 handful fresh basil leaves, shredded

Place the potatoes in a large saucepan with plenty of cold salted water. Bring to a boil and simmer until tender.

Drain the potatoes and mash with a potato masher, then pass through a mouli sieve, if you have one, or failing that, through a fine sieve.

Beat in the butter, oil, and cream. Add the shredded basil leaves and gently mix in. Season to taste and serve immediately.

Following pages: Artichokes and Fava Beans in a Cream and Saffron Sauce

Main Courses

Filled Mushrooms *in their* Golden Cage

Plastic lattice-work cutters are easy to find and cheap but they turn filled mushrooms into an elegant and impressive main course. Remember that mushrooms shrink dramatically in cooking so do buy very large ones, especially if you intend to serve this dish as a main course.

Serves 4

4 large open-cap mushrooms
1 medium red bell pepper
1 small fennel bulb, trimmed and diced
2 tbsp. olive oil
1 tbsp. tamari
$\frac{1}{2}$ tsp. Tabasco sauce
1 scallion, sliced
1 garlic clove, crushed
1 medium zucchini, diced
1 large handful fresh spinach
6 oz./175 g/$\frac{3}{4}$ cup puff pastry
salt and pepper, to taste

Remove the stems from the mushrooms and dice. Broil the red bell pepper until charred black on all sides. Peel, deseed, and then cut into thin strips.

Stir-fry the fennel in 1 tbsp. of the olive oil with the tamari, Tabasco, scallions, and garlic for 2–3 minutes. Remove from the pan and add the zucchini and the mushroom stems. Stir-fry for 1–2 minutes over a high heat. Return the fennel to the pan and cook together for another minute. Remove from the pan.

Add to the empty and almost dry pan the strips of bell pepper and sauté for no more than a minute so they are tinged with black. Return the vegetables to the pan and add the raw spinach and scallion, stirring for a few seconds until just wilted. Season with salt and pepper. Reserve.

Quickly stir-fry the mushroom caps in a little oil and tamari. Fill each of the mushrooms generously with the vegetable mixture and set aside to cool.

Meanwhile, heat the oven to 425°F/220°C. Roll out the pastry on a well-floured surface and roll again, with a lattice-work pastry cutter. Cut into 4-inch/10-cm-square pieces, stretched out to reveal the lattice, and place carefully over each mushroom. Trim excess pastry with scissors. Glaze with beaten egg and bake in the oven for about 30 minutes or until golden brown.

Serve with *Fresh Tomato Sauce* (see page 14).

Scalloped Potato *and* Glazed Onion Tatin

There is not a piece of pastry in sight, so to use the word tatin to describe this is somewhat poetic. It simply refers to the fact that the vegetables are cooked one way up, then turned out, and served upside down in the fashion of the famous upside-down apple tart, Tarte Tatin, named after the Tatin sisters who invented it.

1 lb./450 g/3 cups small onions or shallots   Serves 6–8
¼ cup/60 ml olive oil
1 tsp. bouillon powder
1 tsp. pale brown sugar
1 garlic clove, crushed
4 oz./100 g/1 cup carrots, cut into chunks
3–4 prunes, pitted (optional)
2¼ lb./1 kg/4½ cups potatoes, peeled,
sliced very finely and patted dry to remove excess moisture
salt and pepper, to taste
1 tbsp. very finely chopped fresh parsley

Heat the oven to 400°F/200°C.

Bring a saucepan of water to a boil and plunge in the onions for about 1 minute to loosen the skins. Drain, refresh under cold water, and peel.

Place in a pan with 1¼ cups/300 ml water, the oil, bouillon powder, sugar, and a little crushed garlic. Cover with a lid and simmer for about 10 minutes, checking at regular intervals that the water has not evaporated and adding a little more if necessary, until the onions are caramelized and only just tender. About half way through cooking, add the carrots and the prunes, if using.

Lightly oil or butter a 7-inch/18-cm ring mold or cake pan and tightly pack in the glazed onions and carrots, then the potatoes in overlapping concentric circles, sprinkling with salt and pepper and a little crushed garlic as you work. Cover with wax paper or foil and bake in the oven for about 20 minutes. Then remove the paper and continue to bake for an additional 20 minutes or until the potatoes are tender and beginning to turn crisp on top.

Allow to cool for a few minutes then turn upside down to reveal the shimmering vegetables. Lightly sprinkle with very finely chopped parsley and serve at once.

Mushroom Wellington

This is probably the very first recipe I ever invented, more than twelve years ago. I nearly didn't include it in this book, but nostalgia pulled and tugged and I couldn't resist. I know it is some way from the less-labored vegetarian dishes of today but it does have a festive quality and a balance of flavors that seem to make it a favorite with all who know it. My recipe makes two wellingtons—ideal for a large dinner party. Alternatively, freeze one for a later date. Serve with a mushroom and white-wine sauce, made with finely sliced butter mushrooms, scallions sautéed in butter and finished off with white wine and a drop of heavy cream.

Serves 12

1¼ lb./600 g/2 cups puff pastry
¼ cup/60 ml sunflower oil
1½ lb./700 g/5 cups onions, chopped
4 garlic cloves, crushed
salt and pepper, to taste
1 lb./4 cups whole mushrooms
2 tbsp. chopped fresh tarragon
4 tbsp. soy sauce or tamari
11 oz./325 g/2⅕ cup broken cashew pieces
7 oz./175 g/3½ cups fine fresh breadcrumbs
11 oz./325 g/2⅕ cup ground almonds
1 egg, beaten, for glazing

Roll out the pastry to two rectangles, 11 x 8 inch/28 x 20 cm each.

To make the filling mixture, heat the oil and fry the onions with half the crushed garlic and the salt and pepper for about 20 minutes or until a very dark golden color.

Remove from the pan and set aside. Sauté the mushrooms in the same pan with the rest of the garlic and the tarragon. Halfway through cooking, add the soy sauce and salt and pepper. Set aside, reserving all the mushroom liquor (that is the liquid released through cooking the mushrooms.)

In a food processor or blender, blend the cashew nuts with the reserved liquor to a fine, smooth purée, adding a little water if necessary to make a thick, smooth pâté. Blend the onion mixture until smooth, then blend the mushroom mixture until smooth. Mix all the blended ingredients together in a bowl; add the breadcrumbs and ground almonds. The mixture should hold its shape when formed with the hands.

Heat the oven to 425°F/220°C.

Divide the filling mixture in half; place the mixture in the center of the pastry, to make a long rectangular shape, about 10 inches/24 cm long 2 inches/5 cm wide. With a sharp pointed knife, make diagonal cuts at a 45° angle along one side of the pastry, from the left-hand corner toward the pâté mixture. The cuts should be about ¾ inch/2 cm apart. Repeat on the other side. Fold in the end pieces first. Take a strip of pastry from the left-hand side over the filling, then take one from the right, so they cross over, until the mixture is snugly wrapped up like an Egyptian mummy. Repeat with rest of filling and pastry.

Glaze generously with egg and lift carefully onto a floured cookie sheet, using 2 spatulas or the loose base of a quiche pan. Bake in the oven for 35–45 minutes. To serve, cut into perfect ½-inch/1-cm slices, allowing 2 slices per person.

Braised Fennel (page 75) and *Gratin Dauphinois* (page 95) are perfect accompaniments.

Almond-stuffed Artichokes

6 large globe artichokes **Serves 6**
juice of 1½ lemons
Fresh Tomato Sauce (see page 14) or *Cream and Saffron Sauce* (see page 106), to serve
For the filling
1 cup ground almonds and fine matza meal mixed in equal proportions
2 eggs
1 scallion, sliced
1 medium tomato, diced
a few saffron strands soaked
⅔ cup/160 ml hot bouillon stock
1 tbsp. olive oil
Tabasco sauce, to taste
1 tsp. chopped fresh coriander
1 tsp. chopped fresh parsley
1 piece lemon grass, chopped very finely
1 tsp. *Harissa* (see page 15)
½ a whole nutmeg, grated
2 garlic cloves, crushed
salt and pepper, to taste

Heat the oven to 350°F/175°C.

To prepare the artichokes, trim the stems and remove the tough outer leaves. Bring a large saucepan of water to a boil, together with the juice of 1 lemon, and boil the artichokes for about 20 minutes. Refresh immediately in a bowl of iced water. Then pull out the leaves. Using a teaspoon, scrape away the hairs from the choke and hollow out the heart slightly. Squeeze the rest of the lemon juice over the hearts to prevent them from turning black.

Mix all the filling ingredients together and neatly spoon over the artichoke hearts. Place in an ovenproof dish with 4 tbsp. saffron stock (made by adding a few strands of saffron to ⅔ cup vegetable stock) and 1 tbsp. olive oil. Cover with a lid or foil and bake for 10 minutes, basting at least once. The filling should remain moist, although you may wish to bake the artichokes, uncovered, for 2–3 minutes longer so that they turn a pale golden brown on top.

Serve with a *Fresh Tomato Sauce* or a *Cream and Saffron Sauce*.

Filled Butternut Squash *with* Glazed Pearl Onions *and* Roasted Tofu

I am impressed and fascinated by squash of all kinds, with their often majestic size, their extraordinary, deeply colored protective skins, and their delicious sweet flesh. As the summer ends, and it seems we are in for the long haul of an uninspiring winter, out come these edible sculptures, ready to be turned into all manner of exciting dishes.

Serves 6

For the marinade

3 tbsp. tamari

2 tbsp. olive oil

2 tbsp. water

1 garlic clove, crushed

10 drops Tabasco

10 oz./300 g/1¼ cups firm tofu, cut into 18 cubes

3 butternut squash, cut in half and deseeded

sea salt, to taste

24 pearl onions,
    blanched for a minute to loosen the skins

2 tbsp. olive oil

1 tsp. soft brown sugar

6 tbsp. water

freshly ground black pepper, to taste

6 garlic cloves in their skins

6 oz./175 g/1 cup green beans, topped and tailed

6–7 fresh (wet) walnuts (optional)

2 oz./50 g/¼ cup wild rice,
    cooked in boiling water for 45 minutes until tender

Mix together the marinade ingredients, then place the tofu in the marinade for at least 1 hour to absorb the flavoring. Drain, reserving the marinade.

Heat the oven to 400°F/200°C.

Make criss-cross cuts into the butternut squash flesh, cutting almost all the way down to the skin. Baste the 6 halves generously with half the marinade. Place face down in an ovenproof dish. Sprinkle with salt and bake in the oven for about 30 minutes until the flesh is soft and the skin begins to shrink.

Meanwhile, peel the pearl onions and place them in a saucepan with the olive oil, sugar, water, and salt and pepper. Simmer gently until tender and caramelized. Place the tofu in an ovenproof dish together with the unpeeled garlic and all but 1 tbsp. of the remaining marinade. Bake the tofu for 15 minutes turning it at least once until it is evenly roasted and dark golden in color and the garlic is soft inside its skin.

Meanwhile, blanch the green beans for about 1 minute in salted water. Refresh under cold water. Heat the remaining marinade in a saucepan and quickly sauté the green beans. Add a little more olive oil if necessary.

Finally, fill each half butternut squash with 4 onions, 3 cubes of tofu, and 1 clove of garlic, which each person can peel and mix into the soft flesh. Garnish with the sautéed green beans, the roughly broken walnuts, and a spoonful of wild rice sprinkled over and around.

Spinach Gnocchi *with* Tomato Sauce

These gnocchi (Italian potato dumplings) have nothing at all to do with the little prepackaged bulletlike efforts that go under the same name. They are almost as large as an egg and, unlike the insipid green of the bought variety, these are brightly colored with spinach. You could substitute the spinach with arugula or even nettles for a more sophisticated result. Oh to be an Italian and have these for comfort food!

1 1/2 lb./700 g/3 3/4 cups potatoes, chopped   **Serves 6**
2 egg yolks
4 oz./100 g/1 1/2 cups fresh raw spinach, chopped
salt and pepper, to taste
1/2 cup all-purpose flour
6 oz./150 g freshly grated Parmesan cheese
1 1/2 cups/360 ml *Fresh Tomato Sauce* (see page 14)

Boil the potatoes in plenty of salted water until tender. Drain well to ensure the potatoes are dry, mash them together with the egg yolks, spinach, and salt and pepper while still warm. Beat in the flour and 2 oz./50 g of Parmesan to make a smooth soft dough. Shape into small balls the size of large walnuts.

Bring a large saucepan of water to a steady simmer and drop in a batch of gnocchi. Simmer gently for 4–5 minutes until they rise to the surface. Drain thoroughly. Keep warm while cooking the remainder.

Serve in shallow soup bowls on top of the tomato sauce and sprinkle with the remaining Parmesan.

Following pages: Filled Butternut Squash with Glazed Pearl Onions and Roasted Tofu

Couscous Royale

There are infinite versions of this Moroccan national dish and I feel immensely priviledged to have been brought up with this very specifically Jewish and festive one. I have never come across it anywhere else. The vegetables—seven of them for good luck— are served not only in a savory fashion but sweetened with cinnamon and sugar too. In my childhood days, we ate it not more than twice a year and we considered it a happy treat. It was always a mystery to me that at a traditional Arab banquet, couscous would be served at the end of the meal to make sure that the guests were well and truly satiated. Needless to say they were only ever able to eat a few mouthfuls and the couscous would be as ceremoniously removed as it had been carried in. Couscous is steamed in a couscoussier or you can improvise with a double boiler.

Serves 6
light vegetable stock (see page 12)

6 medium carrots

2¼ lb./1 kg/7 cups pumpkin,
    unpeeled and cut into 3-inch/6-cm pieces

½ small white cabbage, sliced

1 lb./450 g/2 cups chick-peas, soaked overnight

1 onion, left whole

1 bay leaf

1 celery stalk

1 garlic clove

1 lb./450 g/4 cups couscous

1 tbsp. butter

a few saffron strands, soaked in ¼ cup/60 ml very hot water

12 pearl onions

2 tbsp. superfine sugar

just over ½ cup/125 ml sunflower oil

6 medium leeks, cut into 2-inch/4-cm pieces

6 medium zucchini, cut into large chunks

3 oz./75 g/½ cup golden raisins,
    soaked in vegetable stock for 10 minutes

6 medium parsnips, cut into chunks

½ tsp. ground cinnamon

salt and pepper, to taste

Half fill the couscoussier or double boiler with vegetable stock. Cut 5 of the carrots into large chunks and add to the stock along with the pumpkin and cabbage. Bring to a boil and simmer for 5–10 minutes. Then remove the vegetables and set aside.

Meanwhile, place the chick-peas in a pressure cooker with the onion, remaining carrot, bay leaf, celery, and garlic and cook at medium for 20 minutes; or you may also cook chick-peas in an ordinary pan for 1½ hours with 3 cups/750 ml water. (The garlic is not strictly traditional, but with the omission of meat, the chick-peas need additional seasoning.) Drain, discarding carrots, bay leaf, celery, and garlic clove.

Place the couscous in a bowl and moisten with ½ cup/120 ml water, loosening the couscous with your fingers to prevent lumps from forming. Place the couscous in the top half of the couscoussier or double boiler and steam, covered, for 10 minutes. Transfer the couscous to a bowl and, using 2 forks, once again loosen the grains. Return to the steamer for another 10–15 minutes and loosen one final time, this time adding the butter and most of the saffron stock.

Heat the oven to 180°F/350°C.

Add salt and pepper to each vegetable as it is cooked. Place the pearl onions in a heavy-based saucepan with 1 cup/230 ml water, sprinkle with about half the sugar and a little salt and pepper, and sauté until they are golden brown and tender and the water has evaporated. Set aside. Heat 1 tbsp. of the oil in a skillet and sauté the leeks until lightly browned. Remove from the pan. Sauté the zucchini until lightly browned.

Place half the leeks, half the zucchini, and the cabbage in an ovenproof dish with ½ cup/120 ml of the reserved vegetable stock, 1 tbsp. of the oil, 1 tsp. saffron stock, and salt and pepper. Bake for 15 minutes until tender and lightly browned. Place the pumpkin, carrots, chick-peas, pearl onions, golden raisins, parsnips, and the rest of the leeks and zucchini in a second ovenproof dish and sprinkle with the rest of the sugar and the cinnamon. Bake for 15 minutes.

To serve, place the couscous in a high mound on a large round plate and moisten with a little of the stock, reserving the rest to serve separately. I prefer to serve the vegetables separately, but they are traditionally piled on top of the couscous.

Following pages: Couscous Royale

Layered Vegetable Filo Pie

Scrunching the filo pastry like chiffon is all it takes to add a touch of originality to this crisp pie. The colorful layers of broiled vegetables are rainbowlike in effect, making a perfect fare for a summer's day, an alfresco dinner, or a glamorous picnic.

Serves 6-8
1 large eggplant
just over ½ cup/125 ml olive oil,
    plus extra for broiling and oiling
1 lemon
12 sheets filo pastry
1 fennel bulb
1 garlic clove, crushed
Tabasco sauce, to taste
salt and pepper, to taste
2 large zucchini
1 bunch scallions, trimmed
2 red bell peppers
5–6 medium tomatoes, blanched, peeled, and finely sliced

Slice the eggplant into ½-inch/1-cm-thick slices. Sprinkle with salt and leave for about 1 hour to draw out any bitter juices. Rinse well and pat dry. Brush generously with olive oil on both sides and place under a hot broiler until golden brown. Immediately squeeze lemon juice over the hot slices and leave to drain in a sieve lined with two layers of paper towels.

Heat the oven to 425°F/220°C.

Lay half the pastry on the bottom of an oiled 10-inch/25-cm quiche pan, overlapping the pastry so that it is at least 3 layers thick and lightly oiling each sheet with olive oil. Bake for 10 minutes or until a pale golden color.

Meanwhile, slice the fennel into ¼-inch/½-cm slices along the vertical. Mix the remaining olive oil with the crushed garlic, Tabasco, and salt and pepper and brush over the fennel. Broil the fennel for 2 minutes on each side, basting with the oil mixture, until charred and tender.

Slice the zucchini lengthways into ¼-inch/½-cm slices. Baste with the oil mixture and broil until charred on both sides. Baste the scallions and broil whole until charred.

Finally, broil the red bell peppers with no added oil, until the skins are charred on all sides. Allow to cool, deseed, remove skins, seeds, and pith, and cut into quarters. Baste with the oil mixture.

Layer all the vegetables alternately into the pastry case. Cover with one large piece of filo and trim the edges. Cut the remaining pastry into 4-inch/10-cm-square pieces. Scrunch each piece like a piece of chiffon and place closely together on top of the pie to cover completely.

Brush with the oil mixture and bake in the oven at 425°F/220°C for about 15 minutes. Serve immediately.

Gratin Dauphinois

There are probably as many recipes for Gratin de Pomme de Terre à la Dauphinoise as there are cooks who make it. Many use boiled milk and an egg to make the custard in which the potatoes have to cook slowly. Some use onions and some do not. I prefer it with heavy cream, butter, Gruyère, and paper-thin onion. Waxy potatoes produce the best result. Some recipes will advise you to layer the potatoes in neat concentric rings, with neat layers of onion in between, seasoning each layer separately. Years of making this recipe for vast numbers disillusioned me of this elegant notion. I now mix the potatoes, onion, and cream together with all the seasoning in a bowl and pour the lot into a shallow dish, pressing firmly down with the palms of my hands. You will find when cutting into a gratin prepared in this way that the many layers of potato are as apparent as in the more laborious method.

2¼ lb./1 kg/5⅓ cups waxy potatoes   Serves 6
1¼ cups/300 ml heavy cream
pinch of nutmeg
1 garlic clove, crushed
salt and pepper, to taste
2 oz./50 g/½ cup onion, finely sliced
1 tbsp. butter
3 oz./75 g/1 cup grated Gruyère cheese

Heat the oven to 350°F/180°C.

Cut the potatoes very finely by hand into slices about ⅛-inch/3-mm wide. Alternatively, use a food slicer or a food processor. Pat the potato slices dry with a tea towel and immediately mix in the cream, nutmeg, garlic, salt and pepper, and the finely sliced onion. Use the butter to grease an ovenproof dish, about 2½-inches/6-cm deep. Press most of the potato mixture firmly into the dish, finishing up with the reserved slices placed neatly on top. (Make sure that none of the onion is showing or it will burn.) Sprinkle with the grated Gruyère and bake for 1–1½ hours until the top has browned.

Following pages: Homemade Pasta Pouches with Sun-dried Tomato Paste, Ricotta, and Almond Filling

Homemade Pasta Pouches *with* Sun-dried Tomato Paste, Ricotta, *and* Almond Filling

Being a bit of a masochist with an exaggerated sense of the possible, my first attempt at homemade pasta was for eighty people. And not at home for friends but for clients of Culinary Arts, the vegetarian company I set up. That very first time, the pouches lay perfect in their many rows on their many trays, but when I tried to lift them off their floured parchment, almost every one stuck. That experience, enough you would think to put anyone off for life, seemed on the contrary to demystify the process completely for me. The secret is the right flour, the right amount of egg, just the right amount of kneading, then rolling out to the right thickness (I stop rolling only when I am able to read through the thin dough.) Flouring the surface enough but not too much is also vital, as is cooking the pasta in plenty of boiling water in the largest pan you can find and, if necessary, in several batches. Phew! Having said all this, it really is very easy—I promise.

Serves 6

For the pasta
4¼ cups hard-wheat all-purpose flour
6 extra large free-range eggs
2 tbsp. milk, plus 1 tbsp. to help seal the ravioli

For the filling
8 oz./225 g/1 cup ricotta cheese
2 oz./50 g/¼ cup sun-dried tomato paste (see page 11)
⅕ cup fine matza meal
1 tbsp. fresh grated Parmesan cheese
1 garlic clove, crushed
1 tbsp. finely chopped chives
few drops of Tabasco sauce
1 oz./25 g/⅕ cup (about 6) sun-dried tomatoes, finely chopped
1 oz./25 g/⅕ cup red onion, very finely chopped
freshly ground black pepper, to taste

For the sauce
2 cups/460 ml heavy cream
6¹/₂ oz./190 g/¹/₂ cup sun-dried tomato paste
1 cup/230 ml water
5 pieces sun-dried tomatoes
1 tsp. finely chopped chives

To make the pasta, form a mound of the flour on the work surface and make a well in the center. Lightly whisk the eggs and milk in a bowl and slowly pour into the well, gradually drawing in the flour with your hands until well incorporated. Knead the dough for 8 minutes (I time myself exactly). Divide into 6, wrap in plastic wrap, and allow to rest for 30 minutes.

To make the filling, place all the ingredients in a bowl and mix well. Set aside.

To make the pouches, first it is essential that you give yourself enough room to work in. You will need to roll out two equal-sized pieces, side by side, so start with smaller quantities if you need to. Roll out one portion of pasta on a lightly floured surface, using a well-floured thin wooden rolling pin. It is best to keep turning the pasta a quarter turn after each roll and to work in one direction only, away from yourself, so that you are not so much rolling the pasta, as pushing it and stretching it away from you. Lift it occasionally just to ensure that it is not sticking to the surface—if it is, add just a little flour.

Place teaspoonfuls of filling on the pasta leaving a 2-inch/5-cm gap between each mound of filling. Lay a second piece of pasta carefully on top, then press down around the filling with your fingers to seal. Using a 2-inch/5-cm round fluted pastry cutter, cut out the pouches. In order to ensure that the edges are not too thick, press them tightly with your fingers. This is a little time-consuming but really worth the effort. Place pouches on lightly floured plastic trays or boards.

Make the sauce at this stage: Mix all the ingredients except the chives together in a pan and gently bring to a boil. Keep warm.

To cook the pasta pouches, quickly drop them one at a time into plenty of boiling salted water and cook for 3–4 minutes, testing to see that they are tender, cooking evenly, and not falling apart. I personally prefer my pasta very slightly softer than al dente. When the pouches are cooked, drain in a sieve, and very gently turn them out onto a large flat plate. Pour the hot sauce over the pouches and garnish with the remaining chives. Serve at once.

Strawberry Risotto

When a chef recently presented me with a strawberry risotto, I was curious if a little skeptical, but the slightly sweet, gently tangy taste was surprisingly good, the aroma beguiling, and the pale pink color original and tempting. Anyway, strawberries are traditionally—and to brilliant perfection—set off by black pepper, so this risotto takes little to persuade. The red onion is a well-matched addition of my own. Choose firm, deep-red, seasonal strawberries.

1 stick butter   Serves 6
1 large red onion, chopped
1½ lb./700 g/3 cups arborio rice
2 qt./2 lt light vegetable stock (see page 12)
2½ cups/600 ml dry white wine
1 lb./450 g/3⅓ cups strawberries
salt and pepper
1 strawberry, thinly sliced, to garnish
4 oz./100 g/1 cup fresh Parmesan, pared

Heat the butter in a saucepan, add the red onion and sauté until transparent. Add the rice and cook, stirring, for about 2 minutes until the grains are well coated and have become partly translucent.

Meanwhile, in a separate saucepan bring the stock to a gentle simmer. Turn the heat up and add the wine, letting it simmer. Add 1 ladleful of the simmering stock to the rice, stirring constantly. When nearly all of the stock has been absorbed, add another ladleful, always stirring the rice. Continue to add the stock in this way until half of it has been used up. Add half the strawberries, then add the rest of the stock in the same way as before. Add the rest of the strawberries when you have only a couple more ladles of stock to go. (Cooking the rice will take about 18 minutes.)

When the rice is cooked, remove from the heat, add a little salt and plenty of pepper and garnish with the strawberry, fanned out, and the Parmesan shavings.

Sweet Potatoes, Glazed Baby Carrots, *and* Purple-sprouting Broccoli *with a* Yogurt *and* Tahini Sauce

The sweetness of the potatoes and carrots is beautifully offset by the more earthy bite of broccoli and the bitterness—if only hinted at—of tahini.

12 oz./350 g/2 medium sweet potatoes, washed and sliced into ¹/₂-inch/1-cm-thick slices
salt and pepper, to taste
10 oz./300 g/1¹/₂ cups baby carrots, washed and with green tops removed
1 tsp. sugar
1 tbsp. brandy
1 tbsp. butter
3¹/₂ oz./90 g/scant ¹/₂ cup purple-sprouting broccoli, trimmed and separated into 20 small flowerets
2 tbsp. sunflower or almond oil
8 coriander leaves

For the sauce
¹/₄ cup/60 ml plain yogurt
1 tbsp. tahini
1 garlic clove, crushed
8 coriander leaves, roughly chopped

Serves 4

Plunge the sliced potatoes into boiling salted water and blanch for 3 minutes. Drain and set aside.

Place the baby carrots in a heavy-based saucepan together with 6 tbsp. water, sugar, brandy, and butter. Cover and cook gently for 5 minutes, then uncover and cook for a further 2 minutes to reduce the juices by about half. Remove the pan from the heat and set aside.

Blanch the broccoli flowerets in boiling salted water for exactly 1 minute and immediately refresh in very cold or ice-cold water to retain the precious and rare purple color. Set aside.

Heat the oil in a skillet. Fry the potato slices until hot and crisp and golden brown on the outside but soft on the inside.

Add the broccoli flowerets to the carrots. Heat through for just a brief moment. Lay the sliced potatoes in a circle on a large flat plate and top with the carrots and broccoli, reserving the juices.

To make the sauce, strain the reserved carrot juices into the yogurt and stir in the tahini. Add the crushed garlic and the coriander. Give the sauce a good stir and drizzle a little of it over the vegetables; serve the rest separately.

Spinach *and* Pan-fried Tofu *with* Glazed Mango *and* Umeboshi

This is another wonderfully quick dish with enough elegance for a dinner party and enough simplicity for more everyday meals. It has an irresistible flavor—one mouthful and I can guarantee you'll be hooked!
Umeboshi plums are highly flavored pickled plums, salty and astringent, and used in purée form by the Japanese as a condiment over rice and in vegetable sushi. Available from good healthfood stores and Japanese grocers, Umeboshi paste has the added advantage of being incredibly good for you in regulating the stomach's acidity and in this recipe adds a sour note to balance the earthy spinach and the sweet mango.

Serves 6

For the marinade

4 tbsp. tamari

6 tbsp. water

1 tbsp. balsamic vinegar

1 tbsp. finely grated ginger

2 garlic cloves, crushed

2 tbsp. light olive oil

1¼ lb./600 g/2¼ cups firm tofu, cut into 6 slices of equal thickness

2 medium mangoes

1 tbsp. butter, plus 1 tsp. for the spinach

2 tsp. soft brown sugar

2 tbsp. brandy

2 tsp. toasted sesame seeds

2¼ lb./1 kg/12 cups baby spinach

1 garlic clove, crushed

salt and pepper, to taste

pinch of freshly grated nutmeg

18–24 coriander leaves

For the rice

6 oz./150 g/1 cup white basmati rice

1 tbsp. Umeboshi paste

salt and pepper, to taste

Make the marinade by mixing together the tamari, water, vinegar, ginger, and garlic. Place the tofu slices in a dish, cover with the marinade, and leave to marinate for 1 hour.

Meanwhile, cook the rice following this traditional Indian method: Wash the rice in several changes of water and put in a bowl. Pour in enough water to cover it by at least 1 inch/2.5 cm and set aside for 30 minutes. Then drain. While the rice is soaking, bring 8 pt./4 lt water to a boil. Remove water from the heat and add the drained rice. Stir for 30 seconds to prevent it from settling on the bottom. Bring the rice back up to a boil and cook uncovered for 5 minutes. Immediately remove from the heat and drain in a large sieve. Add the Umeboshi paste, lightly stirring with a fork so that it takes on a gentle orange hue. Season with salt and pepper.

Heat the oil in a skillet and fry the tofu slices until they are golden on both sides and begin to very gently crisp up around the edges.

Meanwhile, peel the mangos and with a small serrated knife, cut the flesh from either side of the pit. Slice these two sections into 6 even segments. (There will be flesh left around the pit—scrape this off for use in a purée.) Melt the butter and sugar in a skillet. Add the brandy, then the mango slices and fry over a high heat for no more than 1 minute so they neither fall apart nor lose their glorious color. Stir in the sesame seeds a few seconds before turning off the heat.

Place the spinach, 1 tsp. butter, and the garlic in a saucepan. Sweat with no extra liquid for 1 minute. Remove from the heat. Squeeze out any excess liquid and lightly season with salt, pepper, and a pinch of nutmeg.

To serve, place a small mound of rice on each individual plate. Spoon a sixth of the spinach on top of each serving of rice, then top with 3 slices of the fried tofu, allowing some of the spinach to show through. Finish off with slices of mango. (Any extra mango can be served separately.)

Garnish each serving with 3–4 coriander leaves and serve at once.

Following pages: Spinach and Pan-fried Tofu with Glazed Mango and Umeboshi

Artichokes *and* Fava Beans *in a* Cream *and* Saffron Sauce

This is a sophisticated main course that is made unusual by the addition of raisins.

Serves 6

6 globe artichokes
1½ lemons
1 lb./450 g/3 cups fava beans
salt and pepper, to taste
8 or 9 saffron strands soaked in 1 cup/230 ml hot
   bouillon stock
2–3 garlic cloves, crushed
1¼ cups/300 ml heavy cream
1 tbsp. raisins, soaked in a little warm water
several whole chives to garnish

To prepare the artichokes, cut off the stems and remove the tough outer leaves. Bring a saucepan of water and the juice of 1 lemon to a boil and cook the artichokes for about 20 minutes. Refresh under cold running water, then pull out the leaves and scrape away the hairy choke. Squeeze a little lemon juice over to prevent them from turning black.

Cook the fava beans in boiling salted water for 5 minutes until tender. Refresh under cold running water and slip the skins off. Set aside.

Heat the saffron stock and add the crushed garlic, 1 tsp. lemon juice, and the cream. Cook over a low heat for 8 minutes and finally add the raisins.

To serve, pour the sauce over the artichoke hearts and spoon the fava beans over the top. Garnish with the whole chives.

Green Bean *and* Celeriac Fricassée *with* Chanterelle Mushrooms

Serves 6   1¹⁄₄ lb./600 g/2 cups green beans, trimmed
9 oz./275 g/1¹⁄₂ cups celeriac
4 oz./100 g/2 cups chanterelle or
   other wild or cultivated mushrooms
3 tbsp. olive oil
1 red onion
1 garlic clove, chopped
1–2 tbsp. red wine or water
1–2 tbsp. tamari
few drops of Tabasco sauce
salt and pepper, to taste

Blanch the green beans in boiling water for a few minutes to retain their green color. Refresh immediately in ice-cold water. Set aside. Cut the celeriac into even-size batons, about ¹⁄₂ inch/1 cm x 2 inches/5 cm. Cut the red onion into eighths.

Carefully, with as little water as possible, clean off any dirt clinging to the chanterelle mushrooms. Pat dry with a piece of paper towel.

In a skillet, heat a little olive oil and stir-fry the red onion and garlic until the onion is transparent but still firm. If the mixture dries out, add a drop of red wine or a little water. Add the celeriac and a few dashes of tamari. Over high heat, continue to stir and shake the skillet until the celeriac has softened but retained its shape.

Add the green beans and continue to cook for a few minutes. Add the Tabasco and the chanterelles. These will hardly need a moment to soften—do not overcook otherwise they will lose their exquisite and delicately shaped gills.

Season with salt and pepper and serve immediately.

Following pages: Green Bean and Celeriac Fricassée with Chanterelle Mushrooms

Wild Mushroom Fricassée *with* Glazed Onions *and* Prune Confit

The dish is delicious with soft polenta or mashed potatoes, its deep earthiness softened by these gentler flavors. And the additional sweetness of the glazed onions and prune confit makes this a grand and festive affair.

Serves 6

5 oz./125 g/2 cups dried assorted wild mushrooms

1 tbsp. tamari

1 tbsp. brandy

2 garlic cloves, crushed

2 tbsp. butter

$1/4$ tsp. brown sugar

2 large sprigs fresh tarragon

5 oz./125 g/2$1/4$ cups oyster mushrooms

5 oz./125 g/2$1/4$ cups chanterelle mushrooms, carefully cleaned with as little water as possible

2 scallions, finely sliced

1 tbsp. heavy cream (optional)

For the glazed pearl onions

18 pearl onions

2 tbsp. sunflower oil

2 garlic cloves, crushed

2 tsp. brown sugar

salt and pepper, to taste

For the prune confit

2 oz./50 g/just under $1/2$ cup whole almonds

$1/3$ cup/80 ml sunflower oil

4 shallots or 1 small onion

1 lb./450 g/2$1/4$ cups dried prunes, soaked

$1/2$ tsp. bouillon powder

1 garlic clove, crushed

salt and pepper, to taste

Soak the dried mushrooms for at least 2 hours in 2$\frac{1}{2}$ cups/600 ml warm water, tamari, brandy, and garlic.

Meanwhile, prepare the pearl onions: Place the onions in a saucepan of boiling water and boil for 1 minute. Drain, cool, and peel. Return to the pan, add the oil, $\frac{1}{2}$ cup/120 ml water, garlic, sugar, and salt and pepper. Cover with a lid, bring to a boil, and then lower to a strong simmer for 15 minutes until the onions are soft and browning. Check once in a while that the water has not evaporated, adding a little more water if necessary. On the other hand, if the onions are becoming very soft but there remains too much water, remove the lid and reduce the juices. The onion should end up meltingly soft and a caramelized golden brown.

To make the confit, blanch the almonds in boiling water for 1 minute, then drain, cool, and peel. Heat the oil and fry the shallots until brown. Add the prunes, bouillon powder, garlic, 1 cup/230 ml water, and salt and pepper. Bring to a boil, then reduce to a simmer and cook for 5 minutes. Add the almonds and continue to cook until the water has evaporated and the prunes sit in a thick caramelized onion sauce.

Place the mushrooms in a large skillet and bring to a boil. Reduce the heat to a constant slow simmer and add the butter, stirring continually, then add the sugar. Add the tarragon and continue to cook, stirring occasionally, until the juices reduce by about half.

Remove any tough ends on the oyster mushrooms and gently fold them in, cooking for an additional minute. Carefully fold in the chanterelles and the chopped scallions and cook over low heat for 1 minute. Stir in the cream, if using. Serve at once with the glazed pearl onions and prune and almond confit.

Pastilla

To give the name Pastilla to this pie will be regarded as sacrilegious by the purists. After couscous, this is the national dish of Morocco and in its traditional form it is made with poussin or pigeon, certainly not tofu. But I think my vegetarian version is just as delicious! Try it and see!

Serves 6–8
1 tbsp. bouillon powder
1¼ lb./600 g/4¼ cups plain firm tofu, crumbled into rough pieces
just over ½ cup/150 ml sunflower oil
1 lb./450 g/3¼ cups onions, sliced
½ a whole nutmeg, freshly grated
1 tsp. clear honey
1 egg yolk
8 large sheets filo pastry
2 oz./50 g/⅓ cup whole almonds, roughly chopped
1 scant tbsp. confectioner's sugar
large pinch of ground cinnamon

Dissolve the bouillon powder in 1 cup/230 ml water, add to the tofu, and set aside for at least 2 hours.

Meanwhile, heat the oil, preferably in a stainless-steel skillet, and fry the sliced onion until soft and dark golden brown (pale onion will not give the necessary flavor). Remove half the onions from the skillet and set aside. Add the tofu, including the bouillon it has been soaking in, to the skillet. Fry over a high heat for 15 minutes, allowing parts of the mixture to adhere to the pan and then loosening with a little water. Add the nutmeg and honey and cook for another 5 minutes. At the very last minute, turn the heat off and stir in the egg yolk to add the required richness and succulence to the filling.

Heat the oven to 440°F/225°C.

Lightly oil a loose-bottomed 10-inch/25-cm quiche pan. Line with 4 of the sheets of pastry at right angles to each other, oiling in between each sheet and allowing a generous overhang on all sides. Fill with the tofu mixture, press down, then add the reserved onion and fold in the overhanging pastry. Sprinkle the almonds onto the exposed filling and finally cover with the remaining pastry sheets, tucking them in. Baste with a little oil and bake in the oven for 20–25 minutes.

Transfer from the pan to a large plate and, using a tea-strainer, dust with the confectioner's sugar. Finally, sprinkle with a little cinnamon and serve.

Puy Lentils *and* Broiled Vegetables

For a very long time, lentils, in their various mushy guises or worse still in their undercooked, indigestible pelletlike state, were as inextricably linked in the public's perception of vegetarian food as doorstop leaden pastry and stews of indeterminate origin. What a tragedy! So here's a recipe to salvage the reputation of both. Puy lentils, the new mainstay of today's gastronomic vegetarian restaurants, are absolutely delicious with balsamic vinegar. Here though, they are given a more Middle Eastern flavor. The lemon, cumin, and garlic echo the lentils' own rich, robust flavor.

1 small red onion, cut into large chunks   Serves 6
3 tbsp. olive oil
9 oz./250 g/1 round cup puy lentils
1 tbsp. cumin powder
1 lemon, cut into quarters, plus the rind (zest) of a second lemon
1 garlic clove, crushed
1/2 tsp. Tabasco sauce
1 tbsp. finely chopped fresh coriander
1 tbsp. finely chopped fresh parsley
salt and pepper, to taste
1 lb./450 g/6 cups fresh spinach
For the broiled vegetables
3 zucchini, cut lengthwise into 1/4-inch/5-mm slices
1 tbsp. olive oil for basting
6 red onions, cut into chunks
1 fennel bulb, sliced lengthways into
1/4-inch/5-mm slices
2 red bell peppers
1 yellow bell pepper

Lightly sauté the onion in the olive oil until transparent, then add the lentils, cumin, lemon quarters, crushed garlic, and Tabasco. Add 3 cups/700 ml water and bring to a boil, then reduce the heat and allow to simmer gently for about 25 minutes, adding a little water if necessary. Do not add salt until the end because its absorption slows the cooking process down. When the lentils are cooked—that is, firm to the touch yet tender and not mushy—remove from the heat, add the chopped coriander and parsley and season with salt and pepper.

Meanwhile, broil the vegetables: Lightly baste the zucchini slices with olive oil and broil on both sides until charred. Broil the onions and fennel slices in the same way, adding salt to the fennel. Broil the bell peppers under a hot broiler until charred on all sides, then remove the skins, deseed, and cut into wide strips.

Just before serving, gently reheat the lentils if necessary and quickly stir in the spinach so that it just wilts. Turn out onto a large plate and pile the broiled vegetables on top. Garnish with the lemon rind (zest) and serve.

Baked Mushroom *and* Spinach Risotto *with* Asparagus

Serves 6

2 tbsp. butter
1 large onion, diced
8 oz./225 g/1 cup arborio rice
3 cups/700 ml light vegetable stock
1¼ lb./600 g/5 cups button mushrooms
2 tbsp. tamari
2 garlic cloves, crushed
salt and pepper, to taste
2 tbsp. brandy
1 lb./450 g/2 cups baby spinach
2 eggs, beaten
1 lb./450 g/2 cups thin-stemmed asparagus
2 oz./50 g freshly grated Parmesan cheese

Melt the butter in a saucepan and sauté the onion until transparent. Add the arborio rice and cook slowly, adding stock a little at a time, until it is all absorbed, about 25 minutes. Sauté the mushrooms in a skillet with the tamari, garlic, salt and pepper, and brandy until the mushrooms are tender. Add to the risotto and stir well. Remove from the heat and stir in the spinach. Add the egg and set aside.

Heat the oven to 375°F/190°C.

Blanch the asparagus in plenty of salted water for 1 minute so they are still very firm. (They will soften a little more on baking.) Refresh under cold running water.

Line a 1-lb./450-g loaf pan or a round cake pan with waxed paper. Place the asparagus tightly along the bottom and pour in the mushroom and spinach risotto.

Stand in a roasting pan half-filled with water and bake in the oven for about 35 minutes. Turn out so that the asparagus is on top and serve hot or cold, garnished with the Parmesan shavings.

Sautéed Spinach *and* Smoked Tofu *with* Soft Polenta

An effective combination that looks pretty and tastes great.

For the polenta   Serves 6
1 tsp. salt
12 oz./350 g/just under 2 cups polenta
1¹/₂ sticks butter
7 oz./200 g/2 cups Parmesan cheese, grated
For the spinach and tofu
1¹/₂ sticks butter
4¹/₂ lb./2 kg spinach, washed
1 garlic clove, crushed
small pinch of nutmeg
dash of Tabasco sauce
salt and pepper, to taste
²/₃ cup/160 ml olive oil
1 lb./450 g/4 cups smoked tofu, marinated (see pages 102–3)
and cut into matchstick strips
¹/₄ cup/60 ml soy sauce or tamari
2 tbsp. sesame seeds

To make the polenta, bring 2 qt./2 lt water to a boil in a large saucepan and add salt. Lower the heat to a simmer and slowly add the polenta, stirring with a whisk to avoid lumps. It will soon start to bubble ferociously. Turn the heat as low as it will go and stir regularly with a wooden spoon for about 40–45 minutes until the polenta comes away from the sides of the pan. Stir in the butter and Parmesan cheese.

Melt the butter in a pan and add the spinach, garlic, nutmeg, and Tabasco without adding any additional water. Cook over a low heat, tossing and turning for about 2 minutes, until the spinach is wilted. Immediately remove from the heat, drain off the released liquid and season with salt and pepper.

In a separate pan, heat the olive oil and sauté the marinated tofu strips for 2 minutes, then add the soy sauce and sauté for 3–4 minutes until the tofu is brown and crispy.

To serve, divide the spinach into 6 even portions, twisting around a fork as you would with spaghetti. Divide the tofu and polenta among the plates and liberally sprinkle the sesame seeds over the top and around the sides of each serving.

Following pages: Potato Pastelles with Spinach and Pepper Sauté

Potato Pastelles *with* Spinach *and* Pepper Sauté

I prefer the word pastelle to describe these potato cakes because it has long childhood associations. The pastelles of my youth always had delicious fillings, which were meat-based when I was younger, but became vegetarian as I grew older. Rustic and satisfying, I remember them with joy!

Serves 6–8

2 lb./1 kg/3 cups potatoes, cut into chunks
¼ cup/60 ml olive oil
1 egg, beaten
salt and pepper, to taste
6 oz./175 g/2½ cups baby spinach
2 oz./50 g/¼ cup feta cheese, crumbled
1 garlic clove, crushed
pinch of nutmeg
4 oz./100 g/2 cups mushrooms, sliced
1 tsp. tamari
5 tbsp. fresh breadcrumbs
1 tbsp. mixed fresh herbs (chives, parsley, basil, coriander, or any combination you prefer), finely chopped
2 tbsp. all-purpose flour for dusting
2 cups/500 ml sunflower oil for frying
For the sauté
1 red bell pepper
1 yellow bell pepper
1 lb./450 g/3 cups tomatoes
1 tbsp. olive oil
4 oz./100 g/1 cup red onion, chopped
2 garlic cloves, crushed
8 oz./225 g/3 cups baby spinach
dash of Tabasco
salt and pepper, to taste

Place the potatoes in a large saucepan with plenty of cold salted water. Bring to a boil and simmer until tender. Drain and mash with a potato masher (not a food processor) and add the olive oil.

Add half the beaten egg and season to taste with salt and pepper. Set aside.

Meanwhile, make the spinach and the mushroom fillings: Sweat the spinach in the water clinging to it in a skillet for 1 minute and add the feta cheese, half the crushed garlic, the nutmeg, and salt and pepper. Set aside to cool for a few minutes. Fry the mushrooms in an almost dry skillet along with the tamari and the rest of the garlic. Do not allow to get too soft or wet.

Mix the breadcrumbs with the fresh herbs and set aside.

Divide the potato purée into even-size portions. Dip your hands very lightly in flour, then flatten one potato portion against the palm of your hand. Place a little of one of the fillings in the center, then mold the potato around to enclose it. Pat into a pattie shape, ensuring that the filling is well sealed in. Continue in this way with the rest of the potato and fillings. Dip each pattie in the herb and breadcrumb mixture to coat. Set aside.

To make the sauté, place the bell peppers under a hot broiler until the skins are charred. Peel, deseed, and cut into thin strips. Meanwhile, plunge the tomatoes into a pan of boiling salted water and boil for 1 minute. Set aside to cool, then peel, cut into quarters, and deseed. Heat the oil in a skillet and fry the onion and garlic until just transparent. Add the bell pepper strips and sauté over a high heat for 1–2 minutes. Add the tomato quarters and stir until they begin to soften, then add the spinach. Cook for 1 minute. Season with Tabasco and salt and pepper and remove from the heat.

Heat the sunflower oil in a skillet and fry the pastelles in small batches until they are crisp and golden. Transfer to paper towels and sprinkle lightly with salt. Serve at once.

Following pages: Broiled Vegetable Brochettes with Couscous and a Yogurt and Coriander Salsa

Broiled Vegetable Brochettes *with* Couscous *and a* Yogurt *and* Coriander Salsa

Abundance is the key word here. Cram as many different vegetables, cheese, tofu, even fruit as you possibly can onto each skewer. Be generous with marinades, sauces, and dips and go for the burn. Blackened skins, blistered flesh, charred veggies—these things make a great brochette. Broiling the vegetables before assembling the brochettes may seem time-consuming, but I can assure you that the results are much better.

Serves 6–8

For the sauce
1 heaped tbsp. chopped fresh coriander
2 cups/460 ml plain yogurt
pinch of salt and pepper

1 cup/230 ml olive oil
1 tsp. balsamic vinegar
1 tbsp. tamari
2 red bell peppers
2 yellow bell peppers
4 zucchinis, cut in half,
　　then lengthwise into $1/4$-inch/5-mm slices
8 oz./225 g/2 cups shitake mushrooms or whole large button
　　or chestnut mushrooms
2 heads endive cut into 6 long pieces
1 large fennel bulb, cut into 6 long pieces
6 fresh globe artichoke hearts,
　　or 1 lb./450 g/5 cups canned artichoke hearts
$1^1/2$ lemons
1 large bunch scallions, trimmed
1 large eggplant, cut into thick slices
12 black olives
1 corn-on-the-cob, cut into 6 chunks
12 garlic cloves
2 red onions, cut into 6 chunks
8 oz./225 g/2 cups Haloumi cheese, sliced
7 oz./200 g/just under 2 cups tofu, sliced
　　and marinated (see pages 102–3)
1 lb./450 g/4 cups couscous
sprig of fresh coriander to garnish

To prepare fresh artichokes, cut off the stems and remove the tough outer leaves. Bring a large saucepan of water to a boil, together with the juice of 1 lemon and cook the artichokes for about 20 minutes. Refresh immediately in a bowl of iced water, pull out the leaves, and scrape away the hairs from the choke. Squeeze a little lemon juice over the hearts to prevent them from turning black. For canned artichokes, rinse and drain.

Marinate all the vegetables, except the bell peppers, in the olive oil, vinegar, and tamari for 1 hour. Broil the bell peppers separately until the skins are charred on all sides, then deseed and cut into quarters without removing the skins.

Broil the rest of the vegetables under a very hot broiler, in several batches, until well browned on both sides, and cut into chunks; broil the shitake mushrooms and scallions separately because they will take a shorter time to cook.

Thread the broiled vegetables, cheese, and tofu onto skewers, taking particular care with the corn if you are using wooden sticks. Place under the broiler for just a couple of minutes, turning.

Meanwhile, prepare the couscous either by the traditional method (see page 91) or simply by covering with hot water and allowing to sit for 10 minutes until swollen and soft.

To make the sauce, mix coriander into the yogurt and season with salt and pepper. Serve the brochettes accompanied by the couscous and sauce. Garnish with the sprig of fresh coriander.

Fennel *and* Petit Pois Fricassée

Because of the sweetness inherent in both vegetables, this is one of the most delicate and gentle combinations you can imagine. The cream makes it very rich so, although I would feel fine about serving it as a main course, I would always accompany it with plain cooked pasta or rice.

6 small or 4 large fennel bulbs, cut into quarters   Serves 6
1¼ lb./600 g/6 cups frozen (or fresh in season) petit pois (baby peas)
1 tbsp. butter
2 garlic cloves, crushed
salt and black pepper, to taste
just over ½ cup/150 ml heavy cream
1 oz./25 g/¼ cup freshly grated Parmesan cheese

Braise the fennel as on page 75. Meanwhile, boil the peas in a saucepan of salted boiling water for 5 minutes until tender. Drain, return to the pan, add the butter, garlic, and salt and pepper and toss well over low heat. Stir in the braised fennel and cook together for a further minute. Add the cream and Parmesan and bring to a boil. Serve at once.

Tofu Marsala

It is more effective to cut the tofu in circles but this will cause a great deal of waste so, unless you plan to use it in another dish (for example, Pastilla, page 112) it is fine to cut it into squares.

Serves 6

1 large celery stalk, preferably with leaves attached

6 tbsp. olive oil, plus extra for basting

1/4 small red onion

2 lb./1 kg/6 1/4 cups tomatoes, cut into dice

1 tsp. balsamic vinegar

1 tbsp. brandy

dash of Tabasco sauce

3 garlic cloves, finely sliced

3 tbsp. Marsala wine

salt and pepper, to taste

3 zucchini, cut on the slant, minimum 18 slices

18 garlic cloves, left whole, for the garnish

1 lb./450 g/2 cups tofu, cut into circles 2 inches/5 cm in diameter, or 2-inch/5-cm squares, marinated (see pages 102–3)

4 oz./100 g/1/2 cup Boursin au Poivre or a peppered goats' cheese

For the rice

8 oz./225 g/1 1/3 cups wild rice

1 zucchini, cut into matchstick strips

a little olive oil

juice of 1/2 lemon

1 tbsp. finely chopped fresh parsley

Rinse the wild rice in three changes of water and bring to a boil in 2 1/2 times water to rice. Cover and simmer for 45 minutes, then remove from heat and allow to sit for 15 minutes, until the grain has opened out and is tender. Keep warm.

Heat the oven to 425°F/220°C.

Remove the fibrous threads from the celery and chop neatly. Heat the olive oil in a skillet and sauté the red onion and celery for 2 minutes, then add the tomatoes. Add the balsamic vinegar, brandy, Tabasco, and sliced garlic and cook for a further 2 minutes. Stir in the Marsala wine and simmer for 10 minutes, until the celery is al dente and most of the tomatoes have cooked down to create a thinnish sauce. Season. Add a little water if necessary to remove the sediment from the base of the skillet.

Lightly baste the zucchini slices with olive oil and place under a hot broiler for a few minutes turning until broiled and browned on both sides. Place the whole garlic cloves on a cookie sheet and also baste lightly with olive oil. Place in the oven for about 10 minutes or until the flesh is soft when pricked with the end of a small sharp knife.

Fry the tofu pieces in their own marinade, until golden brown on both sides. (A griddle is ideal for this but a skillet will do.) It's fine to let the skillet dry out and to allow the tofu to char slightly.

To finish off the rice, lightly sauté the strips of zucchini in a skillet, just moistened with olive oil, for absolutely no more than 30 seconds, so they are no longer raw but still completely bright green. Season with a little salt. Mix into the wild rice along with the lemon juice, parsley, and season with salt and pepper.

To serve, arrange a circle of tofu on each individual plate. Heap the celery and tomato on top of it in a mound, allowing the sauce to run all the way around. Top with a roughly broken piece of Boursin and garnish the plate with the zucchini slices and 3 cloves of roasted garlic, opened out. Accompany with the rice.

Pasta Quills *with* Vegetables *and* Mozzarella

Allow the eggplant to soften to make a moist sauce for the fennel. The mix of flavors is about as Italian as they come.

Serves 6
1 lb./450 g/4 cups penne
1 small eggplant
salt and pepper, to taste
1 fennel bulb
$\frac{1}{2}$ cup/120 ml olive oil
1 garlic clove, crushed
dash of Tabasco sauce
8 oz./225 g/1$\frac{3}{4}$ cups ripe tomatoes blanched,
  skins removed and roughly chopped
4 oz./100 g/1 whole mozzarella,
  drained and cut into thin slices
fresh Parmesan cheese shavings and basil leaves, to garnish

Cook the pasta in a saucepan of boiling salted water until al dente.

Chop the eggplant into 1-inch/2.5-cm chunks, sprinkle with salt and drain for about 1 hour to remove any bitter juices. Rinse and pat dry. Chop the fennel into similarly sized pieces.

Heat a little olive oil in a heavy-based pan and fry the eggplant and the crushed garlic quite quickly until soft and golden. Season with Tabasco. (You may need to keep adding a little water to loosen the eggplant, which will stick to the bottom.) Remove the eggplant from the pan and sauté the fennel in the same way. (Softened fennel will lose much of its aniseed flavor but will retain a wonderfully subtle sweet taste.) Return the eggplant to the pan and add the quartered tomatoes, heating for only a minute so the tomato does not completely disintegrate. Add the cooked pasta to the pan and adjust the seasoning. With the heat turned off, add the sliced mozzarella, which will melt gently in the heat of the pasta and make a thread when lifted with a fork.

Garnish with Parmesan shavings and basil and serve.

Baked Celeriac *in a* Saffron *and* Lemon Sauce *with* Gruyère

The celeriac is briefly braised first and then baked, following the same principle as a Gratin Dauphinois. I rarely see the need to eat anything other than a green salad with a dish of such intense richness. Perfect fall fare.

1 large head celeriac
juice of 1/2 lemon
1/4 cup/60 ml olive oil
2 garlic cloves
1 tbsp. butter
3–4 saffron strands, soaked in 1 tbsp. hot water
1 small bunch fresh chives, chopped very small
1 cup/230 ml heavy cream
salt and pepper, to taste
4 oz./100 g/1 1/2 cups Gruyère, finely grated

Serves 6

Peel the celeriac and remove all the woody gnarled parts. Cut into thin, round 1/8-inch/3-mm slices.

Place in a saucepan with 2 cups/460 ml water, lemon, oil, and garlic. Cover with a lid, bring to a boil, and simmer for 7–8 minutes until tender but still firm to the touch. The liquid should have evaporated. (You may need to cook uncovered for 1–2 minutes to achieve this.) Set aside.

Heat the oven to 325°F/160°C. Lightly butter the sides of an oval glass or earthenware ovenproof dish, 10 x 8 x 2 inches/25 x 20 x 5 cm. Arrange the celeriac slices in the dish in concentric layers, until the slices are all used up. Add the saffron water and most of the chives to the cream, season with salt and pepper and pour over the top. Sprinkle with the grated cheese and bake for 40–45 minutes until the cheese is golden brown. Garnish with the remaining chives.

Polenta *and* Eggplant Terrine *with* Tomato *and* Mozzarella

Serve this as a summer lunch accompanied by plenty of mixed-leaf salad. It is best served warm with the polenta still moist and the mozzarella melted. I have assembled this in individual timbales and served them with red bell pepper sauce made from broiled bell peppers, blended with a little water and garlic. You may wish to do the same.

Serves 6–8

1½ lb./700 g/8 cups eggplants, thickly sliced
salt
5 oz./150 g/10 cups polenta
3½ cups/900 ml water
2 oz./50 g/½ cup freshly grated Parmesan cheese
pepper
olive oil for frying and basting
1 tbsp. balsamic vinegar
Tabasco sauce, to taste
1¼ lb./600 g, about 3 large tomatoes
2 garlic cloves, crushed
12 oz./350 g/10 cups mozzarella
3–4 basil leaves, finely chopped

Sprinkle the eggplant slices with salt and let drain for 1 hour to remove any bitter juices. Rinse and pat dry.

Place the polenta in a saucepan and add about half the water. Bring to a boil and simmer gently until the water has been absorbed. Then slowly continue to add the rest of the water, stirring continuously, for about 15 minutes until the polenta is fully cooked and there are no gritty bits left. Add the grated Parmesan and salt and pepper.

Meanwhile, heat the olive oil in a large skillet and fry the eggplant slices on both sides until they are dark brown in color. Place them on a sheet of paper towel to drain and while still hot, sprinkle with salt, balsamic vinegar, and Tabasco.

Slice 2 of the tomatoes thickly and very lightly season with salt, pepper, and a little of the garlic.

Slice half the mozzarella into thick slices and baste with a little olive oil, salt and pepper, and the remaining garlic. Reserve the remaining mozzarella.

Now line a 1-lb./450-g loaf pan with plastic wrap. Place 2 layers of eggplant slices along the bottom, then add a layer of tomatoes, followed by a layer of polenta and one of mozzarella. Add a second layer of eggplant and press down. Turn out when cool. Finely dice the last tomato, mix with the basil leaves and some roughly broken pieces of mozzarella. Sprinkle on top of the terrine, place under a hot broiler until the cheese is melted and serve at once.

Summer Risotto

This risotto is so named because it makes use of two summer vegetables: fresh peas and asparagus. Use the youngest fresh peas and the finest asparagus tips you can find. Anna del Conte, in her delightful book I Risotto, *recommends Vialone Nano for all vegetable-based risotti, and certainly, in this one, I have found it makes a subtle and appreciable difference. If, however, you have difficulty in finding Vialone Nano rice, you can use arborio instead. It is particularly important for this delicate risotto to be almost souplike in consistency, with the rice still firm and tender and with no trace of a chalky center. A sublime dish.*

1 stick butter   Serves 6
2 tbsp. olive oil
4 oz./100 g/⁴/₅ cup onion, very finely chopped
¹/₂ small fennel bulb,
very finely chopped, with the feathery fonds reserved
3 lb./1.4 kg/9 cups fresh peas, shelled
3 qt./3 lt light vegetable stock (see page 12)
1 lb./450 g/2¹/₃ cups Vialone Nano
¹/₂ cup/120 ml light and fruity white wine
1 lb./450 g/2 cups baby asparagus, trimmed to 3¹/₂-inch/9-cm lengths
4 tbsp. chopped fresh flat-leaf parsley
salt and pepper, to taste
6 oz./175 g/1¹/₂ cups freshly grated Parmesan cheese

Melt half the butter together with the olive oil in a heavy-based saucepan. Add the onion and fennel and cook until they are both soft and the palest of gold. Mix in the peas and cook over a low heat for 10 minutes, adding a few spoonfuls of stock during the cooking.

Bring the remaining stock to a boil in another saucepan.

Meanwhile, add the rice to the peas and sauté for 2 minutes, stirring constantly until it is translucent in parts. Add the boiling stock one ladleful at a time, and then add the wine. Stir well and bring back up to a boil. Simmer gently for about 15 minutes (20 minutes if using arborio rice) until the rice is al dente.

Meanwhile, blanch the asparagus in boiling water for 1 minute and refresh under cold water. A few minutes (and only a few minutes, so it does not discolor) before the rice is cooked, add the asparagus to the pan, then the chopped parsley and fennel fonds. Season with salt and pepper. Add the remaining butter and 4 tbsp. Parmesan cheese, reserving the rest to pass around separately.

Filled Fennel *with an* Orange *and* Brandy Sauce

This is so pretty when baked and delicious served with a simple mix of brown and wild rice and a leaf salad to offset the richness of the ricotta. The dish was originally passed on to me by an inspired Israeli potter working part-time in the Crank's kitchen.

Serves 6
3 large fennel bulbs
2 tbsp. olive oil
1 lb./450 g/1 cup leeks, finely sliced
4 oz./100 g/1 cup celery, finely chopped
1 garlic clove, crushed
10 oz./300 g/$^1/_4$ cup ricotta cheese
2 oz./50 g almonds, coarsely chopped
salt and pepper, to taste
1 orange, peeled and cut into 6 slices
Orange and Brandy Sauce (see page 37)
fresh coriander to garnish

Cut the fennel bulbs in half and scoop out most of the insides; reserve.

Blanch the fennel shells in boiling salted water for about 5 minutes until they are just tender (they will cook further in the baking). Refresh under cold water, pat dry with paper towels, and set aside.

Roughly chop the fennel pulp and lightly sauté in the olive oil. Add the leeks, celery, and garlic and continue to fry until transparent. Allow to cool, then mix with the ricotta, almonds, and salt and pepper to taste.

Heat the oven to 375°F/190°C.

Fill the fennel shells with the leek and celery mixture and place in an ovenproof dish with half the sauce. Bake for about 20–25 minutes until the shells are soft to the touch and the filling has begun to brown slightly. Garnish each fennel half with a slice of orange and a sprig of coriander. Serve with the remaining sauce.

Cavatapi *with* Spinach *and* Olives

These springy, corkscrew pasta curls are exactly like a pair of earrings given to me in 1984 by a great friend. I cannot see this pasta without thinking of them both!

salt   Serves 6
3 tbsp. olive oil
1 lb./450 g/4^1/$_2$ cups cavatapi or fusilli pasta
1 tbsp. tomato pesto (see pages 12–13)
4 oz./100 g/^{3}/$_4$ cup black Provençale olives, pitted
2 oz./50 g/^{1}/$_3$ cup sun-dried tomatoes, cut into thin strips
4 oz./100 g/^{1}/$_2$ cup baby spinach or arugula
4 oz./100 g/1 cup feta cheese, crumbled
pepper

Bring a large saucepan of salted water to a boil, add the oil, then the pasta. Bring back to a boil and cook until al dente. Drain thoroughly and return to the pan.

Add the tomato pesto, black olives, and sun-dried tomatoes. Stir in the spinach and heat through until the leaves wilt. Add the feta. Season with salt and pepper, if necessary, and serve at once.

Following pages: Rose Petal Queen Dream

Desserts

Rose Petal Queen Dream

This is one of the easiest things in the world to make! I say this because so many people seem to panic at the mention of the word meringue. Let the freshly crystallized rose petals and the gentleness of rose water tempt you to have a go. You can add a drop of water to the egg yolks, mix them, and freeze for later use in the Strawberry Tart (see page 136).

Serves 12

For the crystallized rose petals
2–3 pink roses, separated into individual petals
3 egg whites, lightly beaten with a fork
2½ cups superfine sugar
For the meringue
12 egg whites
6 cups superfine sugar
1 tbsp. cornstarch
pinch of salt
sunflower oil
For the filling
2½ cups/600 ml heavy cream
1 heaped tbsp. superfine sugar
1 tbsp. good-quality rose water

First crystallize the rose petals by brushing them lightly with the beaten egg white, then sprinkling them generously with the superfine sugar; make sure that the whole petal is well covered and shake off any excess sugar. Place on a cooling rack and allow to dry out completely before storing in an airtight container.

Using a 24 x 10-inch/60 x 25-cm sheet of wax paper, cut out 2 heart shapes using a large heart-shaped pan as a guide, if you have one. If not, fold the paper in half lengthwise draw one half of the heart, cut all the way around and open out. If all else fails, simply draw 2 10-inch/25-cm circles.

Heat the oven to 250°F/120°C.

To make the meringue, whisk the egg whites in a very large bowl on the highest setting of an electric mixer until stiff. With the mixer still running, add the sugar, 1 tbsp. at a time, with a 5-second wait between each new addition. Add the cornstarch and salt halfway through.

Lightly brush the wax-paper shapes with sunflower oil and immediately spread half the meringue mixture over each heart. Don't be too fussy as you do this—the meringues will look even better when standing in rough peaks. Transfer at once to the oven and bake for 1 hour. Allow to cool.

Meanwhile, prepare the filling: Whip the cream and the sugar together until the mixture stands in soft peaks. Carefully fold in the rose water. Turn one of the hearts upside-down onto a large plate. Peel off the paper. Cover with the cream. Turn the second heart upside-down onto a clean plate or cookie sheet, peel off the paper, then very quickly turn it onto the first cream-covered heart. Do not be alarmed if the meringue cracks. (It will be a miracle if it doesn't!) Cover generously with the crystallized rose petals and serve at once. If you need to assemble the heart in advance, reserve the petals and add these only at the last minute.

Tarte Normande *with* Strawberries *and* Raspberries

A version of this tart is served in my favorite delicatessen. Having consumed several slices of it, but never having quite dared to ask for the recipe, I came up with this one. It is as close as can be.

1 quantity *Basic Pie Pastry* (see page 15)   Serves 6
1 lb./450 g/4 cups fresh strawberries and raspberries
1 tsp., plus 2 tbsp. superfine sugar
4 eggs
4 egg yolks
$2^{1}/_{2}$ cups/600 ml cream,
a mixture of $^{1}/_{2}$ light and $^{1}/_{2}$ heavy
$^{1}/_{2}$ cup soft light brown sugar

Roll out the pastry and use to line a 12-inch/30-cm pie pan. Prick the pastry base. Place the tart on a cookie sheet. (I have never yet, in 8 years, succeeded in carrying a full tart over to the oven without spillages so I've learned my lesson.) Arrange the fruit over the base of the pastry case and lightly sprinkle with 1 tsp. of the superfine sugar.

Heat the oven to 400°F/200°.

Whisk the eggs, egg yolks, and the remaining 2 tbsp. superfine sugar together until pale and smooth and doubled in volume. Bring the cream just to a boil and pour into the egg mixture. Mix and pour over the fruit. Bake for 20–25 minutes until the custard is just set. Set aside to cool.

Make the caramel top just before serving: Sprinkle the brown sugar over the surface of the tart and place under a hot broiler. Watch it like a hawk for 1 minute. Remove from heat immediately. The caramel will start to glisten as it hardens.

Strawberry Tart

Every cookbook needs a few favorite classics. This is undoubtedly one of mine and is another steal from my mother's repertoire. You can replace the strawberries with raspberries or other summer fruit.

Serves 8–10

1 quantity *Basic Pie Pastry* (see page 15)
For the filling
just under 1 cup superfine sugar
6 egg yolks
6 tbsp. cornstarch
2 cups/460 ml milk
2 tbsp. cognac
2 lb./1 kg/4 cups fresh strawberries
6 tbsp. apricot jam

Roll out the pastry and use to line a 12-inch/30-cm tart pan. Place the pastry in a preheated 400°F/200°C oven, and bake for 15 minutes until pale gold. Remove from oven and set aside.

Whisk the sugar, egg yolks, and cornstarch together in a heavy-based saucepan, until the mixture holds a ribbon trail for 5 seconds when dropped back into the pan. Bring the milk to a boil and pour gradually into the egg mixture, whisking constantly. Stir the mixture constantly over a low heat until it thickens, moving the spoon right around the edge of the pan so the custard does not stick. Add the cognac and set aside to cool with a piece of wax paper placed over the surface to prevent a skin from forming.

Spread the custard over the pastry base and place the strawberries carefully on top.

Dissolve the jam in a little hot water and pour carefully over the fruit. If you are not serving the tart right away, omit the final step until the last minute.

Indian Baked Cheese Pudding *with* Cardamom *and* Coconut

I was never wild over Indian desserts until I tried this one. The original recipe is from Julie Sahni's Classic Indian Vegetarian Cooking but I have added fresh lime juice to give the pudding a delicious tanginess. I happily serve it to follow spicy Middle Eastern inspired meals and it encapsulates for me the requisites of lightness and richness all in one mouthful. In addition, it provides an excellent opportunity to use a fresh coconut. Make sure it is heavy and shake it to check that it is full of liquid. Then, using a potato peeler or Parmesan flaker, grate the flesh, working quickly to produce a mass of flower petals retaining all the subtle sweetness and fragrance of the coconut.

1½ lb./700 g/3 cups ricotta cheese   Serves 6
¼ cup all-purpose flour
¾ cup, plus 1 tbsp. superfine sugar
seeds from 10 fresh cardamom pods, crushed
juice of 1 lime
4 oz./100 g/1 cup flaked fresh coconut
1 tbsp. butter
rind (zest) of 2 limes

Heat the oven to 165°C/325°F.

Mix the ricotta, flour, ¾ cup/75 g of the sugar, cardamom seeds, lime juice, and one-third of the coconut in a bowl until thoroughly blended. Pour the mixture into a 9-inch/23-cm buttered, square ceramic or earthenware dish. Shake and tap the dish gently until the cheese mixture settles evenly, then sprinkle the remaining coconut over the surface.

Bake uncovered in the center of the oven for 1–1¼ hours until a skewer inserted into the middle of the pudding comes out clean and the top is lightly browned. Cool the pudding thoroughly in the dish, then cover and chill thoroughly in the refrigerator for at least 4 hours or, better still, overnight.

Melt remaining tbsp. of sugar in a pan and quickly toss the lime rind (zest) into it. When it begins to brown, remove from the heat and allow to cool.

To serve, cut the pudding into squares, spooning any remaining liquid from the bottom of the dish over them. Do not be alarmed to see liquid oozing out of the cheese when you first take the pudding out of the oven. As the pudding cools it reabsorbs the liquid and becomes wonderfully moist and crumbly. Spoon the lime syrup over the pudding just before serving.

Eggplant Confites

To me this is an idea that defies all rational expectations. I am fascinated by it. For a truly authentic result, cooking the eggplants three times as described in the recipe is as necessary as it may seem fastidious. Many Moroccan dishes, you will find, ask for and develop one's patience.

Serves 6
3 lb./1.5 kg/12 cups baby eggplants
salt
5 cups superfine sugar
$^{1}/_{2}$ cup/120 ml water
juice of $^{1}/_{2}$ lemon
5 whole cloves
1 large piece ginger
1 cinnamon stick

If the eggplants still have stalks, scrape them, but otherwise leave them whole and unpeeled. Wash thoroughly. Blanch in lightly salted water for 15 minutes, then drain and pierce with a fork to rid them of all water.

Place the sugar, water, lemon, and cloves into a large saucepan. Place over a gentle heat and when the sugar is melted, add the eggplants, one at a time without allowing them to overlap. Simmer gently over a low heat for 1 hour. Remove from the heat and allow the eggplants to cool. Then turn them over carefully and cook for another hour. Repeat the whole process 2 additional times. At the final stage, add the ginger and the cinnamon. The eggplants have to be quite black (not burned), caramelized, and swimming in syrup.

Store in an airtight jar for up to a year.

Fried Pastry Whirls

These are a Moroccan tea-time treat and my grandmother used to make them before my excited eyes. You do have to work quickly and waste no time in eating the faduelos, as they are called in Morocco, to enjoy them while they are still perfectly crisp.

2 large eggs Serves 6
1 tbsp. sunflower oil
2 tbsp. water
1 tbsp. sugar
pinch of salt
1²/₃ cups all-purpose flour
sunflower oil for deep frying
For the syrup
1 cup superfine sugar
¹/₂ cup/120 ml water
orange-flower essence or a few drops of lemon juice

Mix the eggs with the oil, water, sugar, and salt, then add the flour a little at a time. The dough must be soft, malleable, and easy to work with. Knead well for at least 10 minutes.

Cut and divide dough into small balls. With a rolling pin, roll each ball into a long thin strip about 2-inches/5-cm wide. Trim the edges using a fluted pastry cutting wheel and cover with a cloth until all the pastry is rolled out.

Heat the oil in a deep skillet, then lower the heat.

Holding one end with a fork, drop a strip into the oil and twirl quickly around the tines. Drain on paper towels and continue with the remaining strips.

Make a syrup by bringing the sugar, water, and orange-flower essence to a boil. Lower the heat and simmer until it is thick enough to form a thread when dropped from a fork.

Dip each *faduelo* into the syrup or simply pour the whole lot over the pile of pastries. Serve at once.

Chocolate Truffle Cake

Everyone has a favorite chocolate cake recipe and this is my current one—it is quite delicious and very simple to make.

Serves 6 *For the cake*
2/3 cup all-purpose flour
1 tbsp. cocoa powder
1 tbsp. cornstarch
4 eggs
1/2 cup superfine sugar
1/2 stick unsalted butter, melted
For the chocolate truffle filling
9 oz./250 g/2 heaped cups semisweet chocolate, broken into
   pieces
just over 1 1/4 pt./625 ml heavy cream
3 tbsp. brandy
8 oz./250 g/2 cups fresh or frozen raspberries
1 tbsp. cocoa powder

Line the bottom of a 8-inch/20-cm springform cake pan with wax paper, then grease and flour. Heat the oven to 200°C/400°F.

To make the cake, sift together the flour, cocoa powder, and cornstarch into a mixing bowl. In a heatproof bowl set over a pan of hot water whisk the eggs and sugar together. Continue whisking until the mixture is light and creamy and has doubled in bulk. Remove from the heat, add the melted butter, and whisk until cold and thick—when a ribbonlike trail forms on the mixture when some is dropped from the whisk. Very gently fold into the flour mixture.

Spoon into the prepared pan and bake for 30–40 minutes. The cake is ready when a thin skewer inserted into the center comes out clean. Cool and slice the cake in half horizontally. Reserve.

To make the filling, melt the chocolate in a heatproof bowl set over a pan of boiling water.

Whip the cream until it forms soft peaks. Pour half the slightly cooled melted chocolate into the cream and mix well. Add the remaining chocolate and brandy and fold in gently.

Place one round of cake in the bottom of the 8-inch/20-cm springform cake pan. You can freeze the second half for later use.

Pour the chocolate mixture onto the cake and press the raspberries into the mixture, working in rings from the outside in. Refrigerate for at least 1 hour to set.

To serve, wrap a warm, wet tea towel around the outside of the ring and rotate the ring slightly, then lift it off carefully. Dust with cocoa powder.

Chocolate Pecan Tart

I cannot resist this soft and gooey dessert and it is delicious enough to do justice to pecans, which I consider the most beautiful of all nuts. I have a photograph of a huge basket, in the Israeli dining room of a favorite cousin, filled to the rim with pecans, all from a tree in his own yard.

1 quantity *Basic Pie Pastry* (see page 15)   Serves 8

8 oz./225 g/2 cups pecans

For the filling

³/₄ cup superfine sugar

6 tbsp. butter

2 eggs, beaten

1 tbsp. cornstarch

4 oz./100 g/1½ heaped cup semisweet chocolate pieces

1 tsp. cocoa powder, dissolved in a little cold water

Roll out the pastry and use to line a 12-inch/30-cm tart pan. Chop 6 oz./75 g/1½ cups of the pecans.

Heat the oven to 375°F/190°C.

To make the filling, place the sugar and butter in a mixing bowl and beat until light and fluffy. Add the eggs, a little at a time, beating well after each addition. Fold in the cornstarch, chopped pecans, chocolate, and cocoa liquid until well mixed.

Pour the mixture into the pastry case and bake in the oven for 40–45 minutes or until the filling has set. Decorate with the pecans before serving.

Chocolate Caskets *with* a Fig *and* Port Sorbet

I hope you will have a special and romantic occasion to try out these heart-shaped jewel boxes. You could even make sorbets of different flavors and truly fill the caskets with multicolored frozen baubles. The recipe for the sorbet is based on one from that exquisite book, The Roux Brothers on Patisserie.

Serves 6
1 lb. 5 oz./525 g/3¼ cups good-quality semisweet chocolate
a little sunflower oil
For the sorbet
1½ lb./700 g/2¼ cups very ripe fresh figs
½ cup superfine sugar
1⅛ cups/275 ml port
juice of ½ lemon

To make the caskets, melt the chocolate in a heatproof bowl set over a pan of boiling water. Meanwhile, line 6 heart-shaped molds, measuring 4 inches/10 cm across, with foil, pressing firmly against the sides and making the foil as smooth as you can. Brush lightly with the oil and, with a clean brush, paint a layer of chocolate onto the foil. Freeze until set. Repeat a second and third time.

To make the lids, draw around the base of a heart mold on a piece of wax paper 6 times. Oil the shapes lightly and paint with the melted chocolate; freeze until set. Do this another two times, as above.

When the caskets and lids are set, carefully remove the foil and the wax paper. Leave in the freezer until required.

To make the sorbet, peel the figs with a sharp knife, then cut into quarters. Combine the sugar, port, and figs in a saucepan and bring to a boil. As soon as the mixture bubbles, lower the heat and simmer gently for 5 minutes. Remove from the heat and allow to cool completely, then place in a blender together with their poaching liquid and the lemon juice. Blend for 2 minutes and pass through a sieve. Whisk the mixture thoroughly with an electric hand-held mixer. Transfer to a container and freeze. Just before it sets, whisk again and return to the freezer.

To serve, transfer the sorbet to the refrigerator for about 10 minutes before serving, then with a large melon baller, scoop the sorbet into the chocolate hearts and serve.

Caramelized Figs *and* Kumquats *with* Mascarpone *and* Ginger

Kumquats are like miniature oranges, with sweet skins and sour insides. Sometimes they are stuffed full of pits, which you will of course need to remove. Combined with figs, they are both pretty and delicious.

8 oz./225 g/2 cups kumquats   Serves 6
8 oz./225 g/1 1/3 cup dried figs
3 tbsp. warm water
2 tbsp. brandy
2 tbsp. orange juice
1 heaped tsp. soft brown sugar
8 oz./225 g/2 cups mascarpone
1–2 pieces crystallized ginger, chopped

Cut the kumquats into halves or 1/4-inch/5-mm slices. Remove the tough tails from the figs and soak in the warm water, brandy, and orange juice for about 10 minutes until they are a little softened. Transfer the figs and the water, brandy, and orange juice marinade to a saucepan, add the kumquats and sugar and simmer gently for 7–8 minutes until the kumquats are soft but still holding their shape and color. Add a little water or extra orange juice if necessary to prevent drying out and sticking during cooking.

Mix the mascarpone with the ginger and, using 2 tablespoons, form into quenelle shape. Serve with the fruit.

Following pages: Caramelized Figs and Kumquats with Mascarpone and Ginger

Baklava *with* Rose Water

I always imagined that baklava must be terribly difficult to make but this lovely, traditional recipe broke the illusion. I've substituted lime for the more usual lemon juice, and lime rind (zest) to the syrup for a colorful result. You could garnish with crystallized rose petals (see page 134).

Serves 6–8

For the syrup
rind (zest) of 1 lime
2½ cups superfine sugar
1¼ pt./600 ml water
a squeeze of lime juice
2 tbsp. rose water
3 sticks unsalted butter, melted
14 sheets filo pastry
1½ lb./700 g/a little under 5 cups unsalted pistachios, finely chopped

The syrup needs to cool so make it first and refrigerate. First grate the lime using a lemon grater or cheese grater. Boil the sugar, water, and lime juice together in an uncovered saucepan for about 10 minutes. Add the rose water and cook for a few seconds longer. Add the lime rind (zest). Set aside to cool, then refrigerate.

Heat the oven to 350°F/180°C. Brush a large rectangular roasting pan with melted butter and lay half the sheets of filo on top of each other, brushing with melted butter between each sheet and allowing some of the pastry to hang over the sides of the dish. Spread the nuts on top, fold the overlapping pastry over and cover with the rest of the filo tucking in the overlap around the edges and buttering in between each sheet as before. Trim the edges if necessary.

Using a sharp knife, cut the pastry into parallel diagonal lines, about 1½ inches/ 4 cm apart, first from left to right, then from right to left to make diamond-shaped pieces; make sure that you cut right through to the bottom as you go.

Bake for 25 minutes, then reduce the heat to 300°F/150°C and bake for another 25 minutes or until crisp and golden.

Remove the baklava from the oven and pour the syrup over all so that it soaks through the pastry and runs down into the cuts and into the filling.

Set aside to cool, then cut along the same lines and serve.

Candied Fruit

Candied oranges, grapefruit, and lemons are fairly familiar, but baby eggplants, carrots, pumpkin and other gourds, walnuts, and even the tough outer shell of watermelon can also be used to make resplendent preserves. You could do no better than to serve a mixed platter of the jewel-colored fruit and vegetables after a typical Moroccan couscous (much later with coffee or mint tea?) or as festive Christmas sweetmeats. They are traditionally made by Moroccan Jews for Passover when they are served in place of cookies and cakes. They are also made in anticipation of a birth so that the mother and her newly born may be blessed with sweetness.

For the oranges Serves 8
2 perfect, thick-skinned oranges
3 tbsp. salt
1³/₄ cups superfine sugar
just under 1 cup/200 ml water (or ¹/₂ water, ¹/₂ lemon)
For the grapefruit
2 grapefruit
2 cups superfine sugar
1 cup/230 ml water
For the lemons
6 lemons
1¹/₂ cups superfine sugar
³/₄ cup/175 ml water

Grate both the oranges and the grapefruit very lightly so that the peel is not completely removed. Do not grate the lemons at all.

Soak the oranges, grapefruit, and lemons in salted water overnight. Drain. Place in fresh water and bring to a boil. Change the water and boil again; repeat this process once more.

Cut the oranges and grapefruit into wedges and the lemons into quarters. Remove the seeds, cook in three separate pots (because of the different sugar and water requirements of each fruit) with half the relevant amount of sugar and water until tender when tested with a fork.

Remove the fruit from the liquid and add the remaining sugar, in the case of the lemons, waiting until the liquid first becomes clear.

Cook over a low heat until the liquid has thickened and become syrupy in texture. Return the fruit to the pan and simmer over very low heat continually, until the fruit is sitting in a thick, golden brown syrup. Remove from heat, allow to cool and serve.

Following pages: Candied Fruit

Almond Cigars

There cannot have been a single tea party throughout my childhood that did not include these exquisite cigars. A Moroccan delicacy, they are often served with mint tea at the end of festive meals.
You can always use ready-blanched almonds for this recipe, but there is something particularly pleasing about the moist quality of freshly blanched ones, and a pleasure in the flicking, clicking motion of slipping off the skins, especially for this filling, which must not be too dry.

Makes 20 cigars   8 oz./225 g/3 cups almonds, blanched and skins removed

1 cup superfine sugar

finely grated rind (zest) of 1 small lemon

1 egg white, beaten

5–6 sheets filo pastry

2 cups/460 ml sunflower oil for deep frying

For the sugar syrup

just under 1/2 cup superfine sugar

2 tbsp. clear honey

1 tbsp. rose water

Grind the blanched almonds in a food processor together with the sugar and the lemon rind (zest) to release the oils from the almonds and form a fairly coarse paste. (The paste must definitely not be as fine as commercially ground almonds.) Thoroughly mix in one-quarter of the beaten egg-white. Divide the mixture into 20 and roll into even cigar shapes, about 3 inches/7.5 cm long and 1/2 inch/1 cm in diameter.

Cut the sheets of filo pastry across the width into 4 long strips, taking care to keep the pastry covered until you are ready to use it. Lay an almond shape at one end of a strip leaving 1/2-inch/1-cm margin of pastry on either side. Then fold in the bare edges so that the pastry overlaps the almond mixture. Roll up tightly to perfectly encase the paste. Seal the edges with a little oil or water.

To make the sugar syrup, place the sugar in a saucepan and add just enough water to cover the sugar. Heat over a very gentle heat until you can pull a thread from the melted sugar with a spoon. Add the honey and rose water and set aside.

Meanwhile, heat the oil in a deep-fat fryer and fry the cigars in small batches, draining them on paper towels as soon as they are golden brown.

Dip into the sugar syrup to coat and immediately transfer to a lightly oiled cookie sheet. Leave until the sugar syrup is set and has stopped dripping. This is essential or the cigars will stick to any dish you place them on and to each other.

Once dry, transfer the cigars to a serving plate. They are best served fresh but will keep in the refrigerator for a few days, covered with plastic wrap.

Pets de Nonne

In French, the name has a quaintly affectionate ring to it but my mother, who gave me the recipe, cannot help but blush every time someone asks her to translate. Shall we settle for "Nun's Wind" (discretion must stop me from going further) or shall we exercise a little poetic license and call these light-as-a-feather doughnuts "Angel's Breath?" Try serving them with warm caramelized fruit, perhaps pineapple or mango slices, or a Granny Smith apple, sliced into thin rings, quickly tossed in hot melted butter and sugar.

1 cup/230 ml water **Makes about 30–35**
5 tbsp. sunflower oil
pinch of salt
³/₄ cup self-rising flour
6 large eggs
4 cups/1 lt sunflower oil for frying
For the syrup
1 cup superfine sugar
¹/₂ cup/120 ml water
2 tbsp. lemon juice or orange flour water

In a heavy-based saucepan, bring the water, oil, and salt to a boil. Add the flour and stir with a wooden spoon until the dough comes away from the sides of the pan. Remove from the heat and continue to work the dough for a minute longer.

Add 1 whole egg and work until it is thoroughly incorporated into the mixture. Add the remaining 5 eggs, one at a time, mixing well each time. Using a spoon, shape into walnut-sized balls.

Heat the oil in a saucepan until hot, then drop in a few balls of dough. Lower the heat so that they do not begin to brown before having puffed up and risen to the surface. Be careful not to drop in more than a few at a time because they expand in size. Remove and drain immediately on paper towels placed in a colander.

Quickly make the syrup: Bring all ingredients to a boil until the syrup begins to form a thread when lifted with a spoon. Drop in the hot Pets de Nonne, a few at a time, stir to coat, and transfer straight to a serving dish. Serve immediately.

Passion Fruit Ice Cream

The passion fruit of this recipe can be replaced by all manner of other fruit or nuts. The infusion of a vanilla bean to the milk turns the basic custard recipe into a classic recipe for vanilla ice cream. I do not have and have never had an ice-cream maker and for many years have made ice cream, using an electric hand-held whisk, and in quantities very much greater than this.

Serves 6
2¼ cups/550 ml milk
½ cup/120 ml heavy cream
¾ cup superfine sugar
6 egg yolks
juice of 8 passion fruit plus the seeds

Bring the milk and cream to a boil in a saucepan. Place the sugar and egg yolks in the bowl of an electric mixer (or use a hand whisk) and whisk until the mixture becomes thick and white. Gradually add the boiling milk and cream, and return to the pan. Place over a gentle heat and cook until the mixture coats the back of a spoon. Stir continuously and do not allow to boil, or it will curdle. Pass through a fine-mesh sieve and stir occasionally until cold.

Sieve the passion fruit into the ice-cream mixture, releasing all the juices until the seeds are free of any fibrous parts. Clean the seeds under running water and set aside. Pour the mixture into a freezerproof container, cover, and freeze for about 4 hours. When the mixture is nearly frozen, whisk through briskly, and if at all grainy, pass through a fine-meshed sieve; then fold in the seeds and return them to the freezer till set. (I have occasionally repeated this process several times but you may decide that this is a time-consuming luxury.) Remove from the freezer and place in the refrigerator 1 hour before serving.

Individual Crumbles *with* Crème Anglaise

When a classic though usually prosaic dessert such as crumble makes a comeback —admittedly, a touch dressed up and modishly filled with exotic fruit—there are cries of approval throughout the land. Try these individual crumbles made in rings using fragrant English Cox's apple, sweet Indian mangoes, and blue-black pearled blueberries. Put aside morals and qualms about seasonality and local produce, just this once, and enjoy.

1 cup all-purpose flour   Serves 6

1 stick butter, cut into small cubes

just over $^1/_2$ cup superfine sugar

For the filling

6 large Cox's apples or other fragrant eating apples

juice of $^1/_2$ lemon

2 tbsp. butter

a little superfine sugar (optional)

2 large, ripe mangoes, sliced

8 oz./225 g/1 cup blueberries, washed

For the crème Anglaise

3 egg yolks

$^1/_4$ cup superfine sugar

$^1/_2$ cup/120 ml milk

$^1/_2$ cup/120 ml heavy cream

1 vanilla bean

Sift the flour into a mixing bowl. Add the butter and rub together as lightly as possible between your fingers until the mixture resembles breadcrumbs. Stir in the sugar. Reserve.

Heat the oven to 400°F/200°C.

Peel, core, and quarter the apples, then cut into neat slices about $^1/_4$ inch/5 mm thick. Pour the lemon juice over the apples to stop them from turning brown, then place in a nonaluminum saucepan with the butter and a touch of sugar, if necessary. Sauté the apples in the butter over a low heat for about 5 minutes, moving the pan gently so that the apple slices are well coated with the butter and cook evenly.

Lightly grease a cookie sheet with butter and place 6 greased 4-inch/10-cm tart rings on top. (If you do not have rings, use loose-based individual tart pans and lift out before serving.) Divide the apple into 6 and neatly arrange in concentric circles inside each ring. Place the mango slices on top and add the blueberries. Divide the crumble mixture evenly among the rings and bake for about 25 minutes, until the crumble has turned crisp and is pale golden in color.

Meanwhile, make the crème Anglaise. Whisk the egg yolks and sugar with a hand whisk or hand-held mixer until pale and thick. Place the milk and cream in a saucepan with the vanilla bean and heat through until tiny bubbles appear on the surface, then immediately remove from heat. Pour the milk over the creamed egg and sugar. Remove the vanilla bean. Return to the pan and heat gently, stirring constantly until the mixture thickens sufficiently to coat the back of a wooden spoon. Remove from the heat and pass through a fine sieve for silky smoothness. Allow to cool slightly.

Using a spatula, carefully transfer the crumbles, still in their rings, to individual plates. Carefully remove the rings from the crumbles. Pour the crème Anglaise around each crumble and serve at once.

Peach *and* Almond Tart

You can of course substitute just about any fruit for the peaches, including the more usual pears, but I like the contrast of summer fruit's tanginess. If you do use apple or pears, add a couple of tablespoons of Calvados or brandy to the almond mixture.

Serves 8–10

1 quantity *Basic Pie Pastry* (see page 15)
3 sticks butter, softened
1^3/$_4$ cups superfine sugar
12 oz./350 g/2^1/$_4$ cups whole blanched almonds, ground,
   or ready-ground almonds
6 large eggs
5 peaches, unpeeled
crème fraîche, to serve

Roll out the pastry and use to line a 12-inch/30-cm tart pan. Heat the oven to 350°F/180°C.

Mix the softened butter with the sugar in a mixing bowl and beat until the mixture is pale and light. Add the ground almonds and continue to beat for a couple of minutes. Add the eggs, beating them in one at a time.

Cut the peaches in half, remove the pits and arrange the halves on the pastry base. Pour the mixture on top and bake for about 40 minutes. Serve with crème fraîche.

Lemon Tart

I have to include this recipe here. I know it is in just about every contemporary cookbook and practically every restaurant menu—and a good thing too. It is to die for.

For the filling   Serves 8–10
1¹⁄₈ cups/275 ml heavy cream
finely grated rind (zest) and juice of 4–5 lemons
9 large eggs
1 scant cup superfine sugar
1 heaped tsp. confectioner's sugar, to decorate
For the pastry
1 stick unsalted butter, cubed
1¹⁄₃ cups all-purpose flour
1 tbsp. superfine sugar

To make the filling, heat the cream to boiling point. Remove from the heat. Add the lemon rind (zest) and infuse for at least a few hours or even overnight.

Beat the eggs and then lightly whisk them into the cream and lemon mixture. Add the caster sugar to the cream and lemon mixture, then beat the eggs and lightly whisk them into the mixture.

To make the pastry, place the butter in a mixing bowl, add the flour, and work in very nimbly with the tips of your fingers, lifting the crumbs into the air as you work. Add the sugar. Bring the dough together by adding a little ice-cold water. Reserve a small amount of pastry to patch up the cracks that will inevitably appear when it has first been baked.

Lightly butter and flour a 8-inch/20-cm loose-bottomed tart pan. Roll out the pastry on a lightly floured surface and use to line the pan. Prick the pastry all over with a fork and chill for about an hour. Heat the oven to 400°F/200°C and bake the pastry case for 15–20 minutes. Remove from the oven and lower temperature down to 225°F/125°C. Check the pastry case for cracks and patch any with the reserved pastry. Fill the pastry case with the egg and cream mixture and bake for 1–1¹⁄₂ hours until it has set. Do not allow the top to brown in any way and reduce the oven heat if there is any sign of this. Remove from the oven as soon as it is set and allow to cool for a couple of hours. Sprinkle the confectioner's sugar around the edge of the pastry.

Crème Brûlée

Crème Brûlée, *the grownup and so very much more sophisticated relative of Crème Caramel, has become one of the stalwart desserts of the '90s. Serve it in individual ramekins, slightly chilled and with the caramelized top as smooth as a piece of glass. One word of advice: caramelizing sugar is one of life's time-defying devices—don't turn your back on it for even a second. You may wish to flavor the crème with cardamom instead of vanilla or you can always pour it over some fresh berries or sliced bananas before baking. For a nutty flavor, add some pistachios to the gently heating milk and cream or even crush them into the sugar before caramelizing. However you serve it, this dessert is divine!*

Serves 8
³/₄ cup soft brown or superfine sugar
12–13 large egg yolks
½ cup/120 ml milk
½ cup/120 ml heavy cream
1 vanilla bean
³/₄ cup soft brown sugar,
    for caramel topping

Heat the oven to 350°F/180°C.

Mix the sugar with the egg yolks and beat together with an electric mixer at a low speed until thick and creamy. Place the milk and heavy cream in a saucepan together with the vanilla bean and gently heat through—*do not boil*. Remove the vanilla bean.

With the mixer turned on to the lowest speed, gradually add the milk and cream to the beaten egg and sugar mixture. Pour the mixture into 8 ramekin dishes and stand in a roasting pan containing enough water to come halfway up the sides of the ramekins.

Bake in the oven for about 1 hour, or until just set. Remove and immediately refrigerate. Allow to chill.

To make the caramel topping, heat the broiler until very hot. Sprinkle brown sugar evenly over the surface of each ramekin and place under the broiler until caramelized, watching constantly. Chill before serving.

Gooseberry *and* Elderflower Fool *with* a Chocolate Pecan Crust

Use pale pink, sweet summer gooseberries and a fine dark chocolate.

6 oz./175 g/1 cup gooseberries   Serves 6
2 tbsp. soft brown sugar
1 generous tbsp. elderflower cordial
1¼ cups/300 ml heavy cream, whipped
6 oz./175 g/1¾ cups semisweet chocolate, melted
1 oz./25 g/¼ cup coarsely chopped pecans
grated rind (zest) of 1 medium orange

Top and tail the gooseberries with a small sharp knife. Place in a pan with the sugar and heat slowly over a very low heat until the sugar has completely dissolved. Cook for another 4–5 minutes, stirring gently, then break up the softening gooseberries with a fork or potato masher. Remove from the heat and add the elderflower cordial. Allow to cool and fold in the heavy cream.

Divide the fool equally among 6 ramekins and refrigerate for 10 minutes.

Meanwhile, melt the chocolate in a heatproof bowl set over a pan of boiling water. Add the chopped pecans and some of the orange rind (zest) and allow to cool for a few minutes.

Pour the slightly cooled chocolate over each ramekin to form a thin covering layer. Sprinkle the rest of the orange rind (zest) over each and refrigerate for 5–6 minutes until set. Serve cold.

Index